MW01229669

TRUE GRETCHEN

By Steve Carra

Carra Publishing LLC 5220 New Haven Avenue Fort Wayne, IN 46803

For more information, visit www.truegretchenbook.com and stay tuned for True Freedom by Steve Carra.

Printed in The United States of America

1st Edition, 1st Print on Independence Day, July 4th, 2024

1 2 3 4 5 6 7 8 9 10

Softcover ISBN: 979-8-218-45844-7

Hardcover ISBN: 979-8-9910688-1-9

E-Book ISBN: 979-8-9910688-0-2

"Where liberty dwells, there is my country."

~ Benjamin Franklin

TRUE
GRETCHEN

A PARODY BY

STEVE CARRA

Disclaimer

This book is a parody, written by Steve Carra, and the content herein is not authorized by Gretchen Whitmer.

Contents

My Rise to Power

When I meet people for the first time, they are always shocked by how quickly and efficiently I dismantled a once successful and prosperous state. My fans, mostly pinot grigio tipping dog-moms, love to live vicariously through my mega girl-boss era. Meanwhile, my political foes live in fear of which small business owner I'll arrest next. It truly is exhilarating. So just how do I as governor of Michigan find myself in 2024 hovering nearer each day to the once-respected White House? I'm Gretchen Whitmer and this book is about my rise to power.

As a young and ambitious cisgender female, I graduated from Forest Hills Central High School in 1989[1] before attending Michigan State University and Detroit College of Law, ready and eager to make decisions that would impact millions of people.

I know what's best for you, more importantly I know what's best for me, and that's why I ran for office. My father, Richard Whitmer, former President and CEO of a little company called Blue Cross Blue Shield, taught me that corporate elite businessmen can get wildly rich by using the government to their advantage.

That's right, why advocate for the well- being of everyone if you have access in Lansing? And that's when it dawned on me, if businessmen and special interest groups get rich off of connections with the government, what's stopping me from entering politics to ensure people like my daddy can have whatever they want at the expense of everyone else?

With the right mentorship and connections, I knew I could do whatever I wanted. My body, my choice, right? Who cares if my decisions destroy others, as long as they are right for me.

Here's a secret, although my decisions are very destructive for the hard-working middle class, it goes without saying that I don't campaign or make political statements admitting that the policies I seek to implement kick ordinary citizens to the curb. Instead, I tell people that I care about them, believe in the middle class, and enjoy watching people pick themselves up by their own bootstraps. In reality, I enjoy lining the pockets of corporate elitists, you know, my friends who fund my re- election effort. I'm not widely popular because of my ideas, I'm widely popular because I do what the ruling elite wants and I have mainstream media on my side.

A wise person assigned male at birth once said the way to rise to power in politics is in one of two ways, either be willing to sell yourself out or have dirt that you don't want exposed. Special interest groups can manipulate elected officials who are willing to be used or who can be coerced into being used to further their agenda, preferring both.

But which one am I? I've become a female empowerment icon to my progressive base, deceiving them into believing I care about the "marginalized group of the week" trending on TikTok, when in reality my policies suppress people into poverty. I have a proven track record of having a willingness to be used. More importantly, I've learned a special trick, how to coerce others into doing what I want.

You see, not everyone wants to simply be used. Sure, it's easier to be used but it's not as rewarding as using other people. I have mastered the game of politics and am powerful for a reason. It's not because I have good ideas, it's because I deliver ideas powerful people want; it's that simple.

By the time I'm done telling my story, you'll know all that you need to know about me. True Gretchen.

The Man-Made Virus Outbreak

I began my time as governor of Michigan after a glorious campaign victory where I confidently chanted my poll-tested promise to "fix the damn roads." During my first term, I did everything in my power to make sure no one was on the roads. It was part of my illegal shutdown policies. When the man-made virus swept through Michigan, it became necessary to stop the spread by any means necessary, including force. The man-made virus spread quickly; lockdowns were needed in order to halt the progress of the contagion. Obedience was the only choice and the only hope for the people of Michigan, who are too foolish to think for themselves.

Experts were quick to confirm the genius of my central planning policies. People believed Tony Fauci's lie that we needed to "flatten the curve." Bureaucrats like Mr. Fauci created these lies, and the mainstream media ran with the scheme. Every American was urged to take cover in their home. They were told to fear their families, neighbors, and co-workers. I did my part by doing what I do best, digging out another power suit from my girl-boss closet, calling up my botox girl and getting my confident, glowing, and wrinkle-free face back on camera. I would serenely hold court before my subjects, repeatedly reminding Michiganders of the urgency to stop the spread. In parroting the lies of Tony Fauci and the mainstream media, I made my leadership seem necessary. I was on the side of the so-called experts. I acted like shutting down the state was a difficult but necessary choice. That too was a lie. Lives were not saved; they were ruined, lost, and changed forever.

I want to make politics a matter of fear. I know instilling fear within the people makes them more likely to obey. Politics isn't about working out a solution that's best for the people, it means the people fall in line behind their governor and submit to expert rule. Confusion and anger is what I attempted to sow. I was hoping to exploit the emotions of the people so they would relinquish more control to my party and most importantly, me. The people did not need to concern themselves with the impact of the man-made virus; the government is here to protect the people from themselves. That's why they had to isolate and become increasingly dependent on mainstream media narratives.

I imposed mandates for both the shot and mask to extend government power during a time of uncertainty. The mainstream media played their role by lying and instilling fear around the virus instead of promoting real solutions to deal with the problem. This allowed me to take control through executive orders and unconstitutionally push aggressive mandates on the people. Confusion and anger are the result of deceitful communication. This creates an opportunity for central planners to respond to the people's emotions by claiming to have the situation under control. Of course, the situation is not under control. You are under control. That is how central planning works.

The COVID-19 pandemic was indeed a man-made virus outbreak, a pre-packaged Big Pharma special. Big Pharma is not the average special interest. They are a favorite of my friends in the Democratic Party. I offered Pfizer every incentive to operate here in Michigan. That way the jab would never be far from home. It was a win on all sides: my party received Pfizer's lobbying support, Pfizer received government sponsorship for their programs, my deluded super-fans had a shiny new way to virtue-signal, and the people of Michigan shouldered the burden as well as received the shot. This is how my administration works. It works for ruling bureaucrats, and it works for special interests. It does not work for you, but that's of no concern, because the government already knows what's best and doesn't care what you think.

Big Pharma and their experimental jab are what the people need. Really, we should all be thanking Pfizer. They were able to respond to the outbreak of the Wuhan Flu with haste. Everyone who invests in Pfizer deserves recognition for their work in saving public health. I can't help but thank the Chinese Communist Party (CCP), who happens to own a large amount of shares in both Pfizer and BioNTech.[2] Sure, the man-made virus spilled out of a lab in Wuhan, but fortunately CCP leadership was ahead of the game and had considerable financial investment in American pharmaceutical corporations. I also have to thank my friend and mentor Bill Gates, whose philanthropy truly knows no bounds. Mr. Gates believes that there are too many people in the world. He is an expert billionaire who understands that essential population is only that which we can control. Mr. Gates played a significant role in promoting and distributing the jab across the globe and worked to facilitate the relationship between Big Pharma and federal and state governments.[3]

Tony Fauci, Pharma's front man and the initial face of public health, was an asset to Bill Gates. Tony reminded the people to live in fear by forcing them to cover their faces when they were in public. Prohibiting people from being within six feet of one another helped take the human element of affection from society. Our public health initiatives may sound like the rules of a middle school dance, but we promise that we are very smart, and because of our expertise we know these policies are necessary, even if there is insufficient scientific data.

We collude with pharmaceutical special interests in order to create a market in which Pharma giants such as Pfizer can plug and play their products into the lives of the American people for immense profit. I welcomed this strategy to Michigan with open arms. Corporations such as Pfizer needed the man- made outbreak and taxpayer assistance to boost their bottom line. As governor, I did everything in my power to ensure business was booming for Pfizer and other pharmaceutical corporations profiting from the contagion, while the people were subjected to jab mandates.

For an event as serious as the man-made virus outbreak, the numbers must confirm the severity. The presence of other contributing factors was downplayed. This strengthened the narrative that the infection was out of control. Deaths during this time were claimed to have been caused by COVID, even in extreme situations such as motorcycle crashes.[4] Exaggerating the dangers of the virus empowered my claim that drastic measures must be taken to stop the spread. The inflated numbers helped contribute to the public health emergency that I claimed existed. We could not allow society to believe healthy life habits such as getting a proper amount of sleep, taking vitamins, exercising, and reducing stress could help someone's immune system overcome the virus.

I have said "trust the science," however in this case, I controlled the narrative to deceive the public. The authentic, peer-reviewed science indicates that the man-made virus is affected by external variables, such as comorbidities. Studies indicate that comorbidities lead to an increased chance of severe complications from catching the contagion. The study surveyed hundreds of individuals ages 0-24. The most frequent comorbidity was obesity, which was recorded as being present in 19 percent of cases.[5] My regime did not discourage obesity. Blue-haired women on "body positivity" Reddit forums make up a sizable portion of my voter base, and do not like to be told to lose weight. They are not people I want to trigger; thus dieting and exercising were not recommended to help combat COVID-19.

Asthma was recorded in 17 percent of the Fauci virus cases.[6] This data is intuitive, since the contagion targets the respiratory system and asthma already affects the respiratory system, it naturally makes sense that asthma would worsen the condition. However, the data does not serve the political interests of my administration, so it is discarded. The study concluded that when combined with comorbidities, the man-made virus led to greater risk of hospitalization, even for children and young adults. Though the eldest subject in this study was twenty-four years old, the data still demonstrated that comorbidities tend to be more frequent among the older population. If this study was extrapolated to the elderly, it would reveal the undeniable influence of comorbidities on man-made virus cases, something we refrained from advising people to consider in their life habits.

Crippling the Family

Linda, an 85-year-old woman who lived in a nursing home, enjoyed getting visits from her family. Her 60 year old daughter, Sue, wanted to visit her elderly mother, especially during the chaos of early 2021. Sue refused the jab, therefore the government refused her entry into the nursing home. Linda was lonely and missed her family, but this scenario could easily have been avoided had Sue simply complied with government rules. She could have simply obeyed my orders and gotten the jab, as many Michiganders had done, and visited her mother without issue. Though this story and the many others like it may be sad to some, the government needed compliance to protect its people from themselves. This whole situation was Sue's fault, not mine.

Linda was a family-oriented working woman. She was a longtime waitress at the local Coney Island and had spent her entire life surrounded by a loving family. The last two years of her life were spent alone in a nursing home, as her family was forbidden from visiting their mother and grandmother because they had not taken the jab.

Linda's health was not great, but living in isolation away from those she loved the most took an indescribable toll on her well-being. Peering through a window, her family was forced to wave their final goodbyes when Linda passed away.

This story was commonplace in Michigan nursing homes. In the name of health, Linda and her family were separated. As a result, Linda's life was lost too soon, and her family was unable to say a proper goodbye. I'm sure they were comforted by watching my press conferences, where I reminded them that we were all in this together.

Nursing homes received aid as part of my response to the man-made virus. We doled out 48.4 million dollars to Michigan nursing homes.[7] The elderly were vulnerable to covid, so providing funding to nursing homes was of the utmost importance. We believed the best course of action was to quarantine man-made virus patients in nursing homes, especially because infected patients were not strictly separated from non- infected nursing home residents. This made the conditions for "community spread," which is how covid ravaged through nursing homes.[8]

Initially, visitors were banned from nursing homes, but then outdoor, window visits were permitted. Of course, infected patients were allowed to remain where they were.

I gave the nursing homes nearly 50 million dollars, yet the nursing homes accounted for one third of covid deaths in Michigan. One such nursing home, serving the metro-Detroit community, Rivergate, received 356 thousand dollars in aid. During the first wave alone, they reported 55 deaths. Despite the emphasis that more money would be given to the nursing homes who did the best job in keeping the elderly safe, high death rates were common. There were 516 inspection complaints related to the man-made virus, which would equate to over one complaint per nursing home. Of these notices, 149 were for policy failures, but this didn't stop the money flow.[9]

Money is at my disposal, and I decide who gets paid and who does not. There were 26 notices that resulted in no action, but I made certain this was swept under the rug. If every nursing home received the same share, they would each have received approximately 111 thousand dollars.[10]

Matthew, a student studying psychology at the University of Michigan, was eager to receive his degree and enter the workforce. However, his senior year did not proceed as expected, due to the man-made virus. The benevolence of my administration ensured that Matthew could return to school in-person for his degree. However, the jab was necessary. The only way people could safely gather in public spaces was if they were fully vaccinated and my re-election coffers were fully funded by Big Pharma. I was following the science to keep people like Matthew safe. Matthew's senior year was entirely virtual, despite the promises of in-person return, and he was forced to show proof of the jab to retain his status as a virtual student. This was necessary to show full dedication to public health.

From kindergarten to the highest levels of education, the students of Michigan deserved a safe environment. As governor, I implemented school closures, mask mandates, social distancing measures, and jab mandates to provide Michigan students the safe learning environment they required, and teachers' unions the paid vacation time they asked for. Some disagreed, saying things such as the prolonged school closures I championed have set our children back both academically and socially and that we needed local school districts to make decisions they felt were best for their respective communities, and that I was wrong for failing to allow local discretion.

By coercing students into taking the jab, I made it safe for them to resume in-person learning with one another. It has been said that social delays in schoolchildren can be attributed to the man-made virus response. Students could not see the faces of their teachers or their peers, which made social connection challenging. Young children still learning how to read and how to pronounce difficult words could not see their teachers sound out the words for them. They had to rely on listening without any help from their visual learning.

Masks also prevented children from perceiving the emotions of their peers and their teachers. This posed a challenge to learning as well as personal social development. But these children were healthy and protected; they received the jab and were therefore immune to the chilling horrors of the man-made virus.

If these children did truly experience stunted social development, psychologists like Matthew would be there ready and able to help them recover what they had lost. By trusting the science, I set the children of Michigan up for a healthy future, one in which they did not have to make healthy decisions on their own in order to prevent infection from the virus. Teaching kids that the government is here to think for them and that they don't need to think for themselves is a critical aspect of preparing obedient followers of tomorrow.

Included in my illegal shutdowns were churches. This was an especially necessary measure, as churches disregarded the importance of science and public health in their wishes to remain open during the hysteria. This type of blatant resistance cannot be tolerated. Obedience is important. The obedient do not dare resist my dictates. They blindly accept that the government is smarter than them, they know that the experts determine policy and that these experts know what is best for them.

Christians are not obedient. They are organized by families, and they gather in their churches even when they are warned of impending dangers. Do you know how hard it is to control these people? They are immune to our press releases, our policies, and our statistics. They pay no heed to our orders and are seemingly unafraid.

The fearful make for better citizens, they willingly delegate decision-making to the government. We gladly answer their call, and they repay the government through unquestioning obedience. They stayed at home, even while Christians continued to go to church and visit one another's families. The religious believe they rule themselves, that they are independent of the government. This cannot be true, as the government knows what is best and has been democratically selected to rule over all the people. These people need more fear, and only then can they be controlled by our public health mandates.

Public health means that the government decides what is healthy, and the people must obey. Public health is not aided by individual habits or beliefs. A young man in Kalamazoo going to the gym does nothing for our public health. A mom of four choosing organic options for her children similarly does not define public health. Public health policy is determined by the most superior minds in the state of Michigan. Public health means wearing a mask, maintaining six feet of social distance, obeying shutdown orders, and taking the jab as many times as it takes.

There is no merit to a good night's sleep or eating well. Why take vitamin C, vitamin D, or zinc, when you have Pfizer, Moderna, and Johnson and Johnson? These are the options Michiganders truly needed to be healthy. And trust me, the profits on a six dollar bottle of vitamin C are not going to cover the new cabin cruiser my husband's been eyeing! People did not need vitamins, medicines, or healthy habits. Otherwise, the government would have told them their practices were acceptable. In fact, living in fear is helpful for human health. Living in constant fear over the Wuhan Flu causes people to be diligent, to place their trust in science, and to follow my policies.

Good Jobs for Michigan was a program that predated my bureaucratic administration. Pfizer was first in line for Good Jobs for Michigan.[11] The pharmaceutical company's 750 million dollar investment in West Michigan got them an 11.5 million dollar handout.[12] Although Pfizer had not completed their planned project, I lobbied to get them more money.

I want Pfizer here in the state of Michigan, and I am more than happy to commit millions of taxpayer dollars to their cause. I give Pfizer the grants, funded by you, the taxpayers, and then you must get the jab in order to boost Pfizer's bottom line. I manipulate the tax dollars to ensure that large corporations receive kickbacks for their presence here in Michigan.

The doctor-patient relationship had to be destroyed because alternative medicinal efforts such as hydroxychloroquine and ivermectin could not be permitted. The only one-size-fits-all safeguard for the Frankenstein Flu ravaging humanity included the jab, ventilators, and remdesivir. The jab needed a corner on the market in order to receive emergency use authorization status.[13]

The FDA approved Emergency Use Authorization (EUA) status in order to increase the speed of the shot rollout. This made it so jab producers did not have to comply with standard FDA practices in order to bring their product to the market. I had no issue with this process as it was used to facilitate the jab.

However, if rogue doctors attempted to apply similar thinking in providing alternative forms of medicine, such as hydroxychloroquine, they would risk losing their medical license. Doctors who suggested trying alternative measures of their own accord were not in compliance with my central planning, or trusting the science of my pharmaceutical allies. They did not deserve the government stamp of approval. My friends at Pfizer deserved the Emergency Use Authorization status so that the jab could be made available to the masses. We pick the winners, not the marketplace of competing ideas.

When people try to take matters into their own hands, I pull the strings to ensure that my policies are enforced. By threatening dissident doctors and their right to practice, I jeopardized their livelihood and used intimidation to control doctors and patients alike. This is the Democratic understanding of public health put into practice. There is no place for local autonomy or independent, scientific thinking. Science is what we say it is, so light that Fauci prayer candle and obey our government narrative.

Emergency Powers

I activated the Emergency Powers of Governor Act (EPGA) in order to take matters into my own hands responding to the man-made virus outbreak.[14] This act gave me the power to rule by emergency. As any good tyrant would do, I identified the emergency and then reserved the power to respond to it without legislative input.

Some have ridiculed my usage of the EPGA as unconstitutional, but they are commenting from the sidelines and trying to steal my power. I am in charge; I make the rules.

The people of Michigan, including my political opponents, must realize that I know what is best for them. The EPGA aids my central planning initiatives, empowering me to shut down entire sectors of Michigan's economy. This is necessary, so I have said, because I know what is best for the greater good. This is my nanny state, and what I say goes.

My many political opponents attack my reign from all sides. They are unrelenting in their scathing criticisms of my regime. Some, such as the fellows of the Mackinac Center for Public Policy, have criticized my usage of the EPGA and other emergency powers. They proposed their own set of man-made virus rules. The existence of their rules insinuates that mine were insufficient. I take great offense to this, as my central planning rules were successful in lining Big Pharma's pockets and consolidating my own rule in Michigan.

Their second rule claims that the state cannot prioritize particular public health concerns over any other health concerns.[15] On the contrary, this was a public health emergency, and so the only appropriate course of action was for me to assume emergency powers.

Students were confined to their homes, robbed of spending time with friends at school and learning firsthand from the wisdom of Michigan's teachers. For younger children, illegal shutdowns stunted their social development, as well as their cognitive learning. For older students, they were forced to face the world from the isolation of their bedrooms. But clearly, my rules were designed with their safety in mind.

The opposition's criticism also misrepresented my emphasis on the virus, claiming that it was wrong to deem many medical operations as non-essential. I had a narrative to sell; that the Fauci Flu was a grave threat to Michiganders. By categorizing medical services as essential and non-essential, I made my expanded executive power known. I determined what was prioritized. I had the most important voice, so I promoted the causes most advantageous to me.

The Mackinac Center for Public Policy also zeroed in on my use of emergency powers, arguing that my lockdowns were inconsistent and confusing. This assertion may have some substance, but that is not my fault. I believe my practices are clear, and that is good enough. My policies were crafted by experts and bound by progressive principles like science and democracy.

If these principles create any confusion, that is the fault of the confused. They clearly cannot comprehend the principles needed for a democratic society, such as my regime. I used executive orders, emergency powers, dictums posted on my website, and administrative agencies to advance my policies. Who needs the legislature? Who needs the people? I don't, because I know what is best. That power is reserved for me, even if the political system of this state and this country attempt to prevent such tyranny.

Destroying Small Business

My response to the virus generated a political firestorm, mostly from people who were merely attempting to ridicule my decisions for selfish reasons, such as feeding their families. Small business owners improperly believed the lockdowns were a death sentence for their livelihoods, claiming my one-size-fits-all approach ignored the reality on the ground and devastated our local economy.

A selfish Polish immigrant named Marlena Pavlos-Hackney chose to disobey my orders. She knew that forcing people to dine-in at her restaurant Marlena's Bistro & Pizzeria in Holland during a pandemic was intolerable. She was warned she needed to surrender to the authorities by March 18, 2021 or else the State of Michigan would be coming after her for serving food to adults who voluntarily entered her restaurant.[16]

I don't care if someone freely chose to dine at Marlena's restaurant or if she compelled them into her bistro against their will, what this lady did was wrong. Maybe she's used to freedom from her time growing up in Poland decades ago during the Cold War, but this is America and the government has the right to shut her business down if we believe an epidemic exists. Around 5:00 am on Friday, March 19, 2021, state police surrounded Marlena's house, ready to arrest her before she could serve food to more consenting customers.

Attorney General Dana Nessel flaunted her alpha-girl power by unleashing troopers on Marlena and showing not only Marlena but all Michiganders what happens when they don't do what they're told.

Standing in defiance to tyranny is not a good way to stay out of jail. After years of court battles and some time behind bars, Marlena has learned the hard way that freedom no longer exists in America. She would make naive statements like "We don't want this country to be a communist regime that's going to dictate what we can do and what we cannot do."[17] Too late Marlena, this country is ours now.

Marlena seems to think standing against tyranny is a brave and noble cause; personally, I believe she was in it for the money. I have to ask, what truly is important, the health of the people or the bottom line of small businesses who don't cut big checks for my campaigning efforts? I believe it is the health of the people, and so illegal shutdowns were of higher priority than small business greed. A one-size-fits-all approach works because the man-made virus was a one-sized problem. Maybe a handful of small businesses did not survive the virus, but their sacrifice was necessary.

One year after the man-made virus outbreak, my illegal shutdown policies left their full mark on Michigan's economy. In March 2021, 39.7 percent of small businesses reported as closed.[18] A small town that had ten small businesses operating in 2019 would be down to six small businesses in 2021, just under two years into my shutdown policies. Rural towns rely on small businesses to boost the local economy. Small businesses supply jobs to the local populace, and allow people to engage in their local community, whether it be through an ice cream shop or a mom and pop antique store. Local businesses help bring small towns together, whereas my orders isolated communities and forced people apart.

The other 60 percent of small businesses who were able to reopen were immediately saddled by the commands of my bureaucracy. They could not open at full capacity. Sure, I allowed small businesses to open, but I micromanaged the details of their operation to ensure my orders were obeyed. My illegal shutdown policies were a strain on Michigan small businesses, but I had no regard for their problems. My focus was consolidating power, not worrying about the livelihoods and prosperity of local businesses. When it comes to choosing winners and losers, I have no issue making small businesses the big loser, while larger corporations who benefit from my policies are allowed to prosper.

Rick has owned a sandwich shop for over twenty years, nearly all of his adult life, and has been involved with the store since he was born. Rick's dad started the shop in 1960, and the business has remained in the family ever since. They have served the people of Marquette with hand-crafted sandwiches for four decades. Rick and his family have seen it all. They've served sandwiches to construction crews who repaired city streets, they've kept their doors open late to serve busy customers who they treated like family, and they've donated food to the local food pantry in order to give back to the community that gave their family everything. Under my thumb, Michigan took everything from Rick's sandwich shop, but I have no regrets.

Over 50 percent of small businesses reported a negative impact from the economic turmoil I had caused.[19] It was not the virus that made people like Rick close the doors of his business, it was my tyrannical policy. I shut down the businesses to keep communities safe. It is completely within my rights and privileges as lead central planner to determine who wins and who loses in Michigan. It is a job I cherish.

Big corporations such as Blue Cross Blue Shield should be promoted, but small businesses pose a threat to my bureaucracy. Small business owners such as Marlena and Rick truly believe that they know what is best for their business. They have insights into their communities and believe that they are the ones who should voice those beliefs. This is incredibly small-minded because these people are not experts. They may live there, but I have the credentials and the experience to rule over these people with a one- size-fits-all approach. I "follow the science," so I always know what is best. No small business owner, pastor, student, or political opponent, has the capability to rule in the manner I do.

I dropped the central planning hammer on small businesses, but I sympathized with large corporations, who were often aligned with my policy initiatives. Most notably, the jab producers came out ahead. This is fitting since these pharmaceutical corporations produced the entirely-reliable remedy to the man-made virus.

I am all in favor of Pfizer and Moderna cashing in a well-deserved kickback for their role in our public health efforts. These are the winners, two behemoth pharmaceutical corporations. They helped advance my strategy, and in turn, I mandated their product. This is how the government works, a collusion of corporate and administrative interests that results in our profit and your detriment. From 2021 to 2022, when shot distribution was highest, Pfizer generated 75 billion dollars.[20] Don't let these details bother you, you should comfort yourself with the knowledge that we know best how to spend this money.

This scheme was a resounding success, proof of a beautiful partnership in central planning. Moderna trailed behind their Pharma competitor, but still boasted a respectable 36 billion dollars in sales.[21] While thousands of small businesses across Michigan closed their doors, I ensured that Big Pharma could generate record breaking profits. This was public health in practice and evidence that government and big business partnership cares more about providing a quality product than anything else. By implementing jab quotas, public health created wealth for philanthropic corporations. My partners make astronomical amounts of money, and I consolidate power over my subjects by curtailing their rights and forcing a product on them.

My response to the man-made virus outbreak was a concerted effort to invite the progressive forces of the healthcare industry into policy so that the virus could be stopped. I believe that science and health should direct government policy, even if force is required to implement these progressive programs. My idea of health is determined by what the government and their special interest groups deem to be healthy. Not to worry though, as both government and special interests often overlap, but the common denominator is their expertise.

The agencies and lobbies that truly determine policy are staffed by professionals. Since they are experts, there is no reason to question their policy-making, and certainly no reason to question why these unelected individuals are governing the people, as they know what is best for all of us. It is not just experts who make the rules, experts also enforce the rules.

As governor, I am proof of this; my expertise makes me the perfect candidate to do the central planning for Michigan. I used the media to control the narrative of my initiatives. I dressed my deadly policies in friendly language such as "stay home, stay safe," which was my party's framing for illegally shutting down the economy.

I fear-mongered over the virus to discourage Michiganders from exercising their God-given and constitutionally protected rights. I did everything in my power to replace those rights with mandates and fear. I justified my tyranny by explaining that it was for the purpose of "public health," but this term was ironically a mask. Public health masks the sinister agenda of government and special interests to co-opt an individual's right to choose what is healthy and instead forces them to take the Fauci Ouchy.

I call the shots, you get the jab.

Rules for Thee, Not for Me

The man-made virus necessitated restrictions on travel for the safety of all. These restrictions were designed for the people under my rule; it's for their own good. The people needed to stay home and stay safe, because that is the policy I promoted. I elevated science as a new type of authority to justify my illegal shutdowns as being consistent with my preferred scientific studies. However, some travel is necessary, such as when I made the trek to Florida during the man-made virus hysteria. I wasted no time violating my own travel orders. I flew to Florida via private jet, of course, to care for my ailing father who needed my help.[22]

Anyone would have done what I did. My political opponents would have accused me of not caring about my family had I not made this trip. I do care about my family and it is evident that my personal priorities far outweigh those of the people. I am the same governor who enforced social distancing at funerals. I made families visit their loved ones in nursing homes through a glass screen, even if that was their final goodbye. The rules for thee and not for me apply, so I can jet to Florida whenever I see fit.

I was originally going to use my 501(c)4 to pay for the flight, but that wasn't an allowable expense, so instead, I used my campaign account. This was entirely reasonable because I needed security when traveling making it a legitimate expenditure. Reimbursing my campaign account for the equivalent of a first class ticket for myself and my daughters was in order. Although there is no evidence that an agreement was made to fly ahead of making a payment, nobody has been able to prove that I lied.[23]

I went to Florida before I got the shot. In other words, I did not follow my own rules. That is perfectly defensible, given my status. If anyone else tried to do this, they would have been denied. That's the privilege that comes with being the premier state planner.

My dad served the people of Michigan as CEO of Blue Cross Blue Shield, now I serve the people as their governor. If I wasn't able to visit my dad in Florida while he was ill over three years ago, he probably wouldn't be alive. The value of family bonding is critical for the health and well- being of the sick, unless it's regarding the elderly in nursing homes during covid.

The importance of my family is clear, so it's perfectly reasonable for our needs to come before those of the people. I will visit my dad's sunny home in wealthy West Palm Springs any time, but it's alright because I am always the exception to the rule. I use the man-made virus to govern how I see fit, enforcing my agenda with few legal or political barriers. I do not need to observe the same rules, but I assure you I only went to warm Florida for family reasons. You can trust me, surely I would never attempt to deceive you.

The public was not sympathetic; they criticized me for what they perceived to be hypocrisy because I implemented the illegal shutdowns and restricted the rights of law-abiding citizens. I pushed jab mandates, getting in the way of people doing what they wanted and going where they wished. The public had the crazy idea that they had been coerced into restrictive, tyrannical policies while I, their governor, was free to take a vacation whenever I pleased.

This was far from the truth. The rules were made for all, and I observed them. However, I observed the rules when it was convenient for me. That is a privilege afforded to those who make the rules. They are optional. These are the ideas of myself and my colleagues. Why should we obey our own decrees, even if those decrees are public policy? For the people, these policies are mandatory. I am here to make the rules. My constituency is here to follow them. The public should be sympathetic to my personal causes seeing as how I know what is best for them. Alas, it seems no one appreciates tyrannical central planning these days.

Unfortunately, my reasonable explanation was not enough to deceive the public. I was forced to issue an apology. An apology was unnecessary and frankly outrageous. Being above the law, I should not have to apologize to anyone. I deserve a thank you for my benevolent reign. Where would Michigan be without my governorship? I deceived the people of Michigan into thinking my priority was their health by limiting essential freedoms. Claiming dedication to the health and well-being of society, I'll do anything in order to trick the people into believing that I am on their side as a committed defender of democracy. Even though I don't follow my own requirements, that doesn't mean others shouldn't.

In 2021, I caught flak for being spotted at a restaurant eating with my friends.[24] This was over a year after I implemented harsh policies that crippled small businesses throughout the state. This time, I had no compelling reason to explain my hypocrisy. I was caught red-handed, in clear violation of my own rules.

I simply explained that I'm human. I too make mistakes. My explanation may make sense, except for the fact that I don't sincerely believe it. I know I am better than the people who are outraged because I violated my own mandates. The rules don't apply to me, or at least, they shouldn't.

I imposed the policy that limited restaurant parties to six people but because I'm the governor, my party can absolutely have twelve people. I did not follow my own social distancing guidelines, but that's because social distancing was always a method for me to manipulate the people into following my agenda, not my actions. I am immune to tyrannical practices; you, on the other hand, must obey. There are two classes in modern-day Michigan. There are those of us who benefit from the government, fortunately we are the ones in control of the government. The other class is comprised of hard-working Americans who are beneath us. The government exists for us to guide and direct the masses, and in so doing, lining our own pockets.

During the first wave of my illegal shutdown orders, many became frustrated, my husband included. We planned a vacation to beautiful Northern Michigan, hoping to take the boat out for a spin to recharge after such a stressful time of central planning for ten million fools. The boat company would not accommodate us, another example of small business arrogance. They truly believe they can act like they don't know how important my family and I are. My husband even provided a friendly reminder that this was the governor's boat.[25]

They still refused. These small businesses don't understand I am better than they are. I centrally plan this state with expertise. My reward is bad press and no boat time? This is ridiculous, and these types of extreme business practices need to be punished, perhaps through more forceful shutdowns.

Small businesses believe they have independence and that they are free to make their own choices. Not on my watch!

I control when these businesses can open. I control how they operate their business; if they wish to stay open, they must observe social distancing and enforce masking mandates. There is no independence. There is no freedom.

I preside over a bloated bureaucracy, and we decide the rules. My importance should not be forgotten, as the governor of this state and arbiter over your life. If my husband calls ahead to reserve the boat for the weekend, the business should be compelled to comply. Having yet to punish this uncooperative snake for ratting me out, I instead allowed small businesses to open again, albeit with heavy restrictions.

Fortunately for the rest of the people, I displayed mercy despite this one individual who could have further compromised everyone's freedom had I chosen to retaliate. Nonetheless, small businesses shunned me and my family at the first chance they had! Small business owners do not understand policy and they do not know what is best for them. That power is reserved for me, even when boating access is deprived from me.

I have always been transparent when it is politically expedient. I wasn't forthcoming about my trip to Florida, because there was no need to be. As your governor, I may go where I want when I want, even when you cannot. The motive behind my travel is not the business of the people, but the motives of the people to violate my orders is entirely my concern. When I travel, it is for essential purposes. When you travel, it is up to me to decide whether your outing with friends or prayer groups is truly essential. Don't forget that.

The Kidnapping Hoax

My response to the man-made virus left many with pent-up rage. Who would have thought those most outraged would be members and collaborators of the FBI? I am well aware that there are ignorant Michiganders who oppose my reign. I do not know why these people oppose my central planning, as I am bringing them science and democracy. I blame Donald Trump for encouraging such opposition, since no one should ever oppose science and democracy.

I was horrified when I heard of the kidnapping plot against me; at least that's what you would think. Anyone would be scared of a real kidnapping plot against them. Fortunately for me, my good friends at the FBI always had the situation under control. And really, the timing couldn't be better. I'm always looking for a new way to impress the national Democrat Party machine. I used the kidnapping hoax to fear-monger the public regarding my political opponents, namely Donald Trump.

I also used the kidnapping plot as a strategic political point. I immediately tied these extremists to the Orange Man. By making my political opponents out to be extremists, I served my party's political objectives. The year 2020 was a monumental year for my party.

From the illegal shutdowns to mostly peaceful protests in the summer, we schemed on how we could consolidate power and defeat

Donald Trump in the presidential election. Michigan is a battleground state. As a Democrat first and Michigander second, I understood the importance of deceiving the people of this politically crucial state in order to boost Joe Biden's chances of winning the election.

The FBI found that the men they had coaxed into my kidnapping hoax were able to be manipulated into going to great lengths to make a political statement. They know this because they gave these men all sorts of ideas. For whatever reason, these men did not like me to begin with. I'll never understand how people could hate a loving and compassionate governor such as myself, but I know I am better than the people of Michigan. One of the defendants, Ty Garbin, who was among the two who pleaded guilty, in hopes of lighter sentencing, told the jury, "We wanted to cause as much a disruption as possible to prevent Joe Biden from getting into office."[26] Conversely, my goal was to stir up as much disruption as possible to ensure that Joe Biden got into office.

That's why I used the FBI kidnapping hoax to demonize my conservative opposition to try to portray myself and Joe Biden in a favorable light while trying to bring Donald Trump to his knees.

My allies in the FBI were organized and efficient in their control of the narrative surrounding these men. I could learn a thing or two from them on deception methods. Lead prosecuting attorney Jonathan Roth insisted that the kidnappers, "Agreed, planned, trained and were ready to break into a woman's home as she slept with her family in the middle of the night and with violence and at gunpoint they would tie her up and take her from her home."[27] I commend Mr. Roth for his sensationalism as it makes it easier for people to sympathize with me as a clear victim.

There I was, entirely innocent, merely doing my job of controlling the people of Michigan, when all of a sudden these deranged men decided to harm me. They concocted frightening plans under the direction of FBI special agents and informants.

I have no quarrel with the FBI for their contributions to my kidnapping hoax, but I have vehemently denounced the defendants and flagrantly Donald Trump. The conspiracy included wild, attention-grabbing details, such as blowing up a bridge so that law enforcement could not easily help me escape. In fact, it was an FBI operative who suggested the group blow up the bridge. I'm sure the set-up conspirators would have eventually came up with this idea on their own. The FBI agent simply read their mind, so to speak. He got them to admit what they were thinking before they could even think it themselves. When one of the men expressed doubt about the plot, another FBI asset texted him: "Mission is to kill the governor specifically."[28] That part of the plan was a bit intense for my taste, but I will do anything to help the Democratic Party gain control over this country and am proud of the FBI for their efforts.

I saw the harshness of this hoax as a necessary narrative to help spread tyranny throughout the whole nation. The sheer fact that I was used to direct a narrative of this scale gives me standing for consideration as the next chosen leader of our country. Elitists willing, someday I will be selected to occupy the Oval Office and be able to make decisions like our honorable President Joe Biden.

The defendants claimed there was no serious plan to kidnap me. If that were true, then the FBI wouldn't have been so involved in 'thwarting' said plan. The FBI never lies, even if they do pay informants tens of millions of dollars per year. When the FBI says there is a dangerous conspiracy against me, it's true. It's the same thing as me telling the people of Michigan that they have to stay in their homes because of a deadly contagion. Clearly, the feds and I are on the same page when it comes to telling the truth.

Defense attorney Joshua Blanchard described the alleged conspirators as having "no plan," stating "there was no agreement and no kidnapping." The violent extremist who was said to lead the conspiracy, Adam Fox, was described as "practically homeless." He lived in the basement of a Grand Rapids vacuum cleaner shop.[29]

I was the mastermind of my sinister plots from the comfort of the governor's office. Adam Fox, being beneath me in his tactics and status, conspired like a weak man without power.

The defense continued that the identified leader and his friends were too unorganized to carry out such a plot. They claimed that these radicals were "stoned, absolutely out-of-your- mind stoned." Sober minds at the FBI were clearly needed to develop this plot.

Unfortunately, my friends at the FBI encountered some difficulties in the process of the kidnapping hoax. For one, group leader Adam Fox was often inconsistent in how he discussed his federally-aided brainchild. He was known to be noncommittal, consistently opting for more time to plan the hoax.[30] Sometimes he would even consider dropping the plot altogether. What a pansy.

If he had abandoned the plan, what would the feds have done to deceive the public? His bumbling and lack of organization almost ruined the perfect political leverage piece for my Democratic allies.

In an effort to deceive the public, the defense described these delays as predictable, claiming, "The government portrayed Fox, who was commonly dismissed as an indecisive, incompetent, and unserious stoner, as the ringleader."[31]

He was the ringleader because the federal agents said so. Let's not forget these FBI men are experts and anyone involved in entrapping citizens can't be considered the ringleader of the operation. Understanding the situation far better than any member of the public, including the defense attorneys, the FBI deserves our full trust and confidence in this and every matter.

Even experts at the FBI face difficulties. Lead investigator Richard Trask was arrested for domestic violence as the kidnapping hoax was coming together.[32] This was a true shame, losing our lead manager just months before the arrests were finally made. Mr. Trask was convicted of leaving a small bruise on the neck of his wife which caused her to bleed a little bit. Although Mr. Trask's minor crime against his wife was the only instance of violence throughout this entire ordeal, I was obviously at risk of being murdered by the men the FBI was framing.

In spite of this debacle, I still consider FBI agent Richard Trask to be a key ally. Not only was he the lead federal investigator on the case, Mr. Trask was also an ideological ally, sharing my disdain for President Trump. This explains the commitment of his efforts as overseer of the kidnapping hoax up to the point of injuring his wife. Perhaps he took his frustration out on his wife because of how much work was needed from over a dozen FBI operatives in order to bring their scheme to fruition.

On March 28, 2020, Mr. Trask addressed President Trump in the following rant posted on Facebook, "As someone whose wife works in the hospital I hope you burn in hell along with your douchebag [effing] reality tv star. His ego is going to kill a lot of people and anyone who supports that is a dumbass. This is what you get when you elect an egotistica[l]/narcissistic maniac to the top office. He needs people to be nice to him or he won't help. [Eff] you douche."[33] Harsh language, but Mr. Trask was an ally of my regime as well as the Democratic Party.

Make no mistake about it, the FBI and I are on the same team. We share the same ideology. We agree we must discredit President Trump, as well as anyone who opposes our beliefs. We agree that the kidnapping hoax serves our interests by portraying me as a helpless victim and demonizing Donald Trump by falsely associating him with the alleged conspirators. I agree with the FBI, the deep state should keep power, that way special interests can best steer our political system.

I knew Joe Biden was the right choice for president, as his corruption is befitting for the Democratic Party. We agree that deceiving the people is a necessary objective, and we will continue to do so at every turn.

As an establishment politician, I fully understand the importance of never letting a tragedy go to waste. When the FBI goes to great lengths to cook up an entrapment plot on me, it is my job to make sure it becomes a political wildcard.

The arrests for my kidnapping hoax were made in October of 2020. Coincidentally, this was a perfectly timed tragedy, and it was foiled at an even more opportune time. What a spectacular string of coincidences. With the 2020 presidential election looming, I was able to sow confusion and deceive the public into thinking right-wing terrorism was a culpable movement. In fact, this almost gift-wrapped incident entirely obscured the actual terrorism of the "mostly peaceful" protests over the summer. I used the kidnapping hoax against me to aid the campaign of President Biden, and directly attacked Donald Trump by drawing up completely baseless connections between him and the alleged conspirators. Some have called me the "Jussie Smollett of governors," which I can only assume is a compliment.

I take issue with Donald Trump's involvement in this matter. These men had no real connection to Mr. Trump, as they were loosely associated with a fringe, anarchist political ideology. But still, anyone to the right of me politically is a MAGA extremist and complicit in the plot against me.

These several men planned the kidnapping hoax, but the millions of people who support Mr. Trump and conservative causes fueled their fire through rhetorical warfare. Words can hurt.

At a rally following my kidnapping, Mr. Trump's supporters shouted "lock her up!" in reference to me. Why should I be locked up? I am the victim. Federal agents entrapped fringe political persons to entertain the idea of kidnapping me. Clearly I was in grave danger from a stoned group of wanna-be soldiers. Why does this have to happen to me? I am the governor!

Is everyone so quick to forget my service towards my party? The people I believe should be locked up are those who don't follow my orders. Additionally, the conspirators should have received hefty prison sentences for being sabotaged by the FBI.

It seemed like a winning strategy, one that was familiar; control the narrative, deceive the people, and ensure everyone falls in order. This is the featured strategy in the Democratic playbook. The FBI is familiar with executing this type of strategy as well, so it seemed a foregone conclusion that the forces of unpatriotic central planning would prevail yet again.

The failure of the kidnapping hoax was unthinkable. The jury should not consider the evidence, or lack thereof; the jury should remember their governor has an agenda to push. The agenda is to further Democratic consolidation of power, both in Michigan and at the federal level. Sadly, the jurors did not understand this; they needed more expert management from their governor.

The collapse of the persecution of the defendants in my kidnapping plot is described as "one of the biggest embarrassments for the FBI's counterterrorism and informant programs since 911."[34] It truly was an embarrassment, not because my federal allies did anything wrong, but because this strategy is a proven winner.

The FBI wins nearly nine out of ten terrorism cases, boasting an 88 percent conviction rate. Entrapment is tough to argue in court, so using entrapment as a means of advancing the Democratic cause of deception seemed to be a sure-fire victory.

Manipulating the public requires weaponization of narratives, which is exactly how I handled the kidnapping hoax. The conspirators came from a variety of backgrounds, coming from as far as Delaware to wage terror against me. The connection between a resident of

Delaware and the conspiracy hoax can only be explained by one factor, the FBI.

The FBI devised the plot knowing it would grab headlines in the mainstream media. This plot was meant to disturb public opinion right before the November 2020 presidential election. The FBI recruited people who would willingly entertain extreme rhetoric, and people who did not like me or my party. I'm not sure how they found people who would dislike me, but they needed these people to use as pawns. The FBI was so committed to stopping the kidnapping plot against me that they drove one of the men from Delaware to Michigan, just so they could keep a closer watch on him. Their commitment to my safety is astounding.[35]

What's even more remarkable is their devotion to deception, as they were able to manipulate these men into finally agreeing that action should be taken. The FBI was in control the entire time. The hoax became a nationally known political ploy when the plot culminated just prior to the election. The men involved were easy scapegoats, taking the fall for the operation of my friends.

However, blaming these men was insufficient. Public sympathy would side with me, but it wouldn't stop there. With the assistance of mainstream media, the propaganda deceived America into believing our deception. This kidnapping hoax needed to instill fear into the people and that it did. The people of Michigan, and of the United States, needed to blame conservatives for the violent behavior of the radical left.

It also demonstrated the necessity of the FBI, who seemed to successfully stop the plot when in reality they were the ones who contrived it all. The public did not need to know the FBI was the guiding force of the hoax.

To stoke the flames of fear across the nation and take this hoax to the federal level, I publicly condemned Donald Trump in an article for the *Atlantic*. Mr. Trump was responsible for a plot that he had no awareness of, and no connection to. I wrote, "Ever since Donald Trump first stepped foot in the White House, we have moved away from the common ideas and values that are supposed to unify us as a country, putting leaders across the country, including me, in danger."[36] It was President Trump who put me in harm's way, even though I was never in any danger whatsoever.

In a display of Olympic-level mental gymnastics, I was able to correlate Donald Trump with a ragtag, stoned squad of wannabe-militants who were duped into scheming against me. I accused President Trump of taking America away from common ideas and values, but I gave no concrete definition of what these values might be.

My party defines common values as whatever we say they are. Everyone has to follow our rules. The Democratic idea of unity is one of common misery. I elaborated in my *Atlantic* article, "From the White House all the way down to state and local governments, these leaders have shown a disdain for unity and have failed to rally fellow Americans against a common enemy: COVID-19."[37] Common values means instilling fear over the man-made virus instead of educating the public about the value of healthy life habits. My party believes that living in fear is more important than freedom. Mr. Trump did not want the people to be afraid of the election infection. We couldn't have that. Therefore, the vast Democratic deep state and uniparty operatives went to work in bringing down Donald Trump, instilling fear over his very existence. Thanks to the FBI, Mr. Trump and his supporters were falsely connected to the men tricked into the kidnapping hoax. The people are either obedient, which is desirable, or they are all potential conspirators. Opposing me is siding with Mr. Trump, which also somehow means siding with anyone who does something we don't like.

The FBI picks and chooses who and what they investigate. They're selective about which responsibilities they execute in their job.

They're just like me in that regard. I choose to abuse my executive powers when it serves the interests of my party. However, when it comes to working with the legislature, I am much more selective on how I do my job, if at all.

The FBI chose not to do their job in the investigation of the voter registration firm, GBI Strategies.[38] In October of 2020 there was substantial evidence of election fraud in Muskegon. The presidential election was only a month away, so nefarious activity involving voter registration should have been seen as a serious concern. However, when trying to cause chaos and confusion, election interference is a useful tactic. We need deceased and out-of-state residents to vote in order to secure our democracy.

Once again, my friends at the FBI decided to pick and choose their battles. FBI Director Christopher Wray let the case sit for years. I am so proud of Director Wray for bravely choosing inaction. He could have faced serious backlash for ignoring concerns of election fraud, but he stayed true to the path of deception. My fellow girl-boss cohorts, Secretary of State Jocelyn Benson and Attorney General Dana Nessel, did the same, choosing to turn a blind eye to election fraud. Unfortunately for Secretary Benson, she is a repetitive election lawsuit loser having lost seven election lawsuits. I'm proud of her for standing strong despite losing over and over again.

The kidnapping hoax was the perfect piece of political ammunition to stir up the media against any and all opposition. Donald Trump was the most prominent political scapegoat. The men charged with attempting to kidnap me took the fall for this staged event, but it was Mr. Trump who we were after most. By portraying these men as Donald Trump sympathizers, we made it seem like Mr. Trump was somehow involved.

I immediately capitalized on the rhetoric in my article with the *Atlantic* by saying, "He is sowing division and putting leaders, especially women leaders, at risk. And all because he thinks it will help his reelection."[39] See how easily I can deceive the public through my abuse of the mainstream media? In one sentence, I portrayed the sitting President as a figure who was actively targeting Americans, harming women, and only doing so for cheap political gains.

I did this all by implicating him in a plot with which he had no involvement. The whole article was a ruse as a matter of fact. It was projection on my part as I sought cheap political gain by using the kidnapping conspiracy against Mr. Trump. I turned the set-up into an asset, which had been planned by my friends at the Bureau. I wanted to influence this election by skewing voters towards the left. Even when I am not in the race, Democrats must win.

Indoctrination Camps

Imagine a place where deception reigned. In this place, confusion was valued to the highest degree, not because confusion presented an opportunity for growth or true learning, but because confusion allowed for the perfect chance to produce obedience. Imagine the power of deception within this place, where authority could masquerade its false promises as true, and in doing so create many people who have no proper understanding of who they are or what they could become. In this place, pretending is encouraged. The leaders act as if they are the practitioners of good government, but they are only petty tyrants. This place of deception and indoctrination is widespread. Enter a Michigan public school classroom, otherwise known as an indoctrination camp.

My illegal shutdowns radically changed education in Michigan. Masks became the mandatory new dress code in Michigan's schools. Pre-schoolers and college students alike all were compelled to wear masks, that is if they were allowed to attend in-person school.

Little Addison, a kindergartener at the time of the man-made virus outbreak, went through some of her most formative years under my masking mandates. Addison had to learn her letters while muzzled by the mask. She could hear her teacher enunciate words, and watch her teacher write out letters and words on the board. But, Addison struggled with phonetics. She needed to see her teacher's face as she sounded out letters and words.

Addison needs to get with the times and watch a YouTube video on enunciation. After all, these were uncertain times, and my expertise dictated that Addison was better off illiterate than exposed to a virus that primarily affected the elderly and obese. I made sure Addison was insulated from any threat of a normal life through mask mandates and social distancing. All of these controlling policies were enacted in the name of safety, but it came at the cost of Addison's educational development. It was a necessary sacrifice for my future career goals that will set Addison back for the rest of her life.

Not only did Addison's performance in the classroom suffer, but her social development was greatly impeded by my edicts. Kindergarten marked the first time that Addison was consistently around other children her age for an extended period of time. I forced all these kids to wear masks. Instead of seeing the faces of their new friends, kids like Addison could only tell the color of their masks. Addison liked to wear a pink mask. Her friend liked to wear a blue mask. What they learned about one another was superficial and incomplete.

It was difficult for Addison to connect with her classmates. She could not see their expressions, their smiles, or see the faces they made when they were laughing at a joke or were upset about something. Addison became confused, and still struggled to connect with her peers. Despite lacking the academic proficiency or skills necessary for success in the classroom and in social environments, she was moved through the grades. This is the product of the government attempting to blot out the naturally healthy experience of seeing the faces of others and learning appropriate emotional responses.

Social distancing and living in fear is actually healthy for kids, especially in their formative years. There are people who would try to say that my policies stunted our children's development. Who cares about reading, writing, and arithmetic anyway? Those are outdated lessons. I took one from George Orwell's playbook and turned kids into Junior Spies.

Kids today have iPads. They have all the tools necessary to learn the lessons that truly matter, such as what I say. The kids should learn how smart their governor is. They should read about how I kept them safe by doing irreparable damage to their developing brains. They should learn the holy pillars of intersectionality and the rainbow flag jihad.

Covid offered the perfect opportunity to control the subject matter of school curriculums in Michigan. In place of the old useless lessons, which do not instill fear or obedience among the children, progressive allies have introduced further Diversity, Equity and Inclusion (DEI) initiatives.

The United States of America has always been about equality. However, COVID-19 enabled my allies to shift from the old understanding of equality, which held that every citizen was entitled to God-given rights, to equity. Instead of focusing on natural rights that allow all to exercise their freedom as they reasonably see fit, equity forces the people to obey the state by determining outcomes.

Race has been the perfect vehicle to ram the equity narrative down everyone's throat. Racism was on life support until it was revived by the Marxist Black Lives Matter movement.

It worked, Americans are now conscious of their race again, and they use this to guide their beliefs on relations with other races. Under progressive equity, there is no unified identity as Americans, rather there are categories of Americans. It is the job of progressive officials, such as myself, to pick winners based on equity principles.

DEI actively encourages a victim mentality within its believers. Not to worry, we in the government are here to empower the victim mindset. We choose how people are treated based on who has been most victimized, even if the crime was against their ancestors centuries ago, or in some cases, nonexistent. The divisiveness of DEI is the perfect counter-strategy to equality's unity, as equity spreads faster and more effectively than any man-made virus. Equity tears people apart, creates resentment, and makes them more attracted to the helping hand of the welfare state.

I have been happy to see that Michigan has embraced critical race theory in its schools under the guise of other names. This curriculum introduces children to division, racial resentment, and victim mentality, all of which are certainly beneficial for them. Instead of teaching children division using quotients, I prefer to use division within discriminatory hiring or educational quotas.

Our progressive school superintendents, such as Nikolai Vitti in Detroit, ensure kids are well prepared for indoctrination. The superintendent said, "We're very intentional about creating a curriculum, infusing materials and embedding critical race theory within our curriculum." To echo Mr. Vitti's sentiment, this is indeed a very intentional effort. It's not enough to control whether they wear masks or get jabbed; the government must also control what the children believe. Mr. Vitti continued, "Students need to understand the truth of history, understand the history of this country to better understand who they are and about the injustices that have occurred in this country."[40]

Students must base their understanding of themselves and others on the tenets of critical race theory. They need to learn terms such as oppressor and victim. It's this style of divisive rhetoric that keeps people like me in power. The victors write history, and I'm attempting to parlay my victory in the gubernatorial race to help the progressives rewrite the history of this nation.

The effects of DEI education are evident in school districts throughout the state. This educational virus has many devotees, and we are all trying to control the kids. A first grade teacher set the foundation for brainwashing kids by telling six and seven year olds, "Anti-racist education is patriotic education. #1619 Project."[41] This is a common talking point, equating equity programs with true patriotism. This makes race baiting seem like a necessary component to America.

A fifth grade teacher took to Facebook to resolve internal conflict, "I have an immense amount of straight, white privilege. And I need to do what's right for kids."[42] Here's an example of an adult who was successfully indoctrinated. Divisive instructions in equity led this teacher to resenting the color of her own skin, instilling within her a pervading guilt that informed every aspect of her worldview. Since her job is being an educator, this guilt drives her to spread this resentment to her students.

In a classroom that is undoubtedly sanitized, the potent parasite of equity germinates through its many forms including self loathing, white guilt, victim mentality, and indoctrination of children. We also divide girls against boys. A few of our best-loved phrases are "Girls rule the world" and "The future is female." This message serves to ensure the boys feel less confident and able to lead, and that the girls grow up to be a reliable girl-boss voting bloc for my eventual White House run.

Political opposition has protested progressive policies in schools. They claim this is not education, but indoctrination. Would an indoctrination camp be as colorful and inclusive as Michigan classrooms? Rainbow flags mark many Michigan classrooms, demonstrating the state mandate for inclusion, even at the cost of discomfort.

Decorating the political agenda in rainbows is an attempt to deceive the kids into accepting the new normal, the normal that is decided by political leaders and activists. The same principles that brought the alphabet brigade and rainbows to your child's classroom were those of Alfred Kinsey, an instrumental figure for the sexual revolution. Mr. Kinsey's ideas are the foundation for modern sexual education programs for children. The records of Alfred Kinsey's studies were thoroughly investigated, and it was discovered that there was, "Criminal experimentation on children funded by taxpayers."[43]

Believing all humans are sexually driven, Mr. Kinsey proudly studied the use of manual and oral techniques on little children, finding that a baby as young as four months could have an orgasm. His studies also revealed an eleven month old baby was able to have ten orgasms in a one hour period.[44]

Ideological colleagues of mine found Mr. Kinsey to be suitable for children's sexual education. This is because Mr. Kinsey used his authority as a scientist to hide the horrors of his experiments. Sound familiar?

This was a massive cover-up of repugnant acts in the name of science, and people believed it because they trusted the science. The report referenced Mr. Kinsey's contributions and "Provided the 'scientific' foundation for America's sexual revolution."[45] He brought science to sexuality, which had formerly been seen as a private matter to be taught in the family and by religious beliefs.

Science is necessary for our democracy. Perverse science brought sexuality into the public sphere as a guise for people like Mr. Kinsey to abuse children with immunity. His legacy lives on as the LGBT movement is fostered in Michigan classrooms, a policy of which Mr. Kinsey would be in full support.

The LGBTQ indoctrination movement not only enjoys full support at the state level, they also receive support from the federal government, including from Congresswoman Elissa Slotkin. Congresswoman Slotkin represents Livingston County and areas in metro-Detroit. Her top aide, Mona Shand, patrols the county as the "eyes and ears" for her boss. Mona sits on a diversity council, which is committed to teaching critical race theory in schools. Her objective is to deceive kids into forming their identities in terms of victimhood.

Congresswoman Slotkin and Mona not only support this mentality in terms of race, but also in sexuality.[46] Where would the children of Michigan be without their teachers and elected officials sponsoring curricula that manipulate every aspect of their identities? Kids need to learn that the state is their greatest beneficiary, and they must understand this during their most formative years. Congresswoman Slotkin participated in reading *I am Jazz* to schoolchildren, a book on transgenderism. I applaud her efforts to indoctrinate our kids into being more inclusive, particularly for enabling those pretending to be something they are not.

School districts have gleefully absorbed the government's desires for indoctrination over education. Farwell Schools of Clare County developed an entire system in case even one individual student decided to lie about their gender. They call this system the "Gender Support Plan.[47]" A more appropriate title would be Gender Enforcement Plan, as the plan reinforces gender ideology on confused and impressionable children.

Once a student enters the Gender Support Plan, they are safely in the hands of the experts. The school assigns both a counselor and an administrator to manage the case. The counselor and administrator instigate the child's pretend exercise, claiming that science has supported their decision to feed into the child's dysphoria. The school district does so without the child having to show proof of suppressing their hormones or mutilating their body.

The school standards state, "Make a good faith effort to make the appropriate changes regardless of whether the student has transitioned, sought a legal name change, or taken other legal or medical action."[48] Enabling dysphoria by any means necessary, this is a policy I can endorse.

The school also reserves the right to withhold this information from parents. They cite child safety, to which all sane parents would agree that their children are most safe listening to whatever

Hollywood and the experts at their school tell them to believe. In fact, parents only interfere in the indoctrination process. They do not know what is best for their own kids. It is the responsibility of the government and the school districts to discover what curriculum is best suited for controlling the students.

At Gull Lake Community Schools, the alphabet brigade was hard at work to deceive kids regarding their biological identities. An AP Literature teacher often took to social media to express support for far left causes, including equity for sexual orientation.[49] AP Literature teachers are supposed to be preparing high school students to read at the college level, learning how to critically engage with a text. However, I much prefer the pretend-approach. Place teachers who believe that biology is malleable in the classrooms and let them influence the kids.

Many high school teachers are also the leaders of their school's Gender and Sexuality Alliance. These types of clubs are common in Michigan schools and we need more of them. Gaslighting the children into believing that they can ignore nature is important for their growth and development; whichever identity they pretend to be magically becomes their reality.

After deceiving students into believing that sexuality is an advanced scientific phenomenon, the state lets them do whatever we want. They don't need their parents. They don't need God. They have their teachers, they are organized into alliances, and above all else they know that the nanny state is here to mutilate their bodies.

Coordinating an indoctrination camp requires experts. Thankfully, ideologues at the University of Michigan developed the TRAILS program, which is a curriculum seeking to change the way children perceive their identities. This is necessary work. Kids cannot be themselves or else they will be hurt from all the brokenness in this world caused by the government eroding Christianity and the nuclear family. Although the government is responsible for causing the problems, we like to appear as the saviors.

Kids must be whatever made-up version of themselves they want to be after being exposed to state-sponsored gender and racial indoctrination. The TRAILS curriculum is highly effective in promoting this agenda, and can be summarized well by the Identity Wheel.[50] The first prompt asks children to consider which identities they think about the most. The wheel haphazardly presents potential identities on a chart depicting many options. One could presumably spin the wheel and land on an identity that has been engineered by the government.

The categories include race, gender, sexual orientation, sex, socio-economic class, among others. It truly is double or nothing. The categories are suitable for adults, containing content inappropriate for children. Instead of focusing on positive traits children may possess such as kindness or courage, the identity wheel steers children toward sexual and leftist minded thoughts and ideas. This is by design.

We don't need independent thinking, courage, or true kindness from our kids. We need children to understand that they can pretend to be any gender they want, and their government will support them in their confusion and make them feel popular and brave.

A basic form of identity children ought to focus on is the color of their skin; that way they can know if they have been oppressed, or if they have privilege and need to repent. The TRAILS program helps the government control the children through indoctrination, manipulating people in their most formative years by selectively teaching understandings of identities that serve our political purposes.

I take issue with those who disparage my openness to inviting LGBTQIA clubs and teachers into Michigan classrooms. My opponents, both political and cultural, advocate for traditional approaches to sexuality. They claim the most important piece of science regarding sexual education is that abstinence is the only foolproof way to avoid teen pregnancies. That clearly isn't true, as pharmaceutical special interests have paid my colleagues millions of dollars to push birth control on young women, disrupting their hormones and oftentimes leaving them with mental health issues.

Other forms of protection are also dressed up in the guise of a peer-reviewed journal and sold as nearly one hundred percent effective. If two teenagers have a pregnancy they are unprepared for, I personally have fought hard to make sure they have every opportunity to terminate the life of their child through abortion.

All of these solutions are proof of the science, proof that a class of managing experts, headed by me of course, know what is best for the children of Michigan. My opponents believe that Christianity and the family have a right to educate their children. Who said that those are their kids? Those children are Michiganders, and I am the governor of Michigan meaning they belong to me.

My political philosophy demands that I interfere in the development of children and expose them to indoctrination. Christianity's ethics threaten my idea that identity can be whatever is pretended, and destroys my importance as a tyrant. The family stands in the way between me and the kids.

When parents take initiative in their child's education, it is more difficult for me to indoctrinate them. That's why I believe in taking rights away from parents and transferring them to the government so that central planning of the mind may continue unabated.

The Elliott Larsen Civil Rights Act of 1976 introduced an expansive list of qualities that were banned from public discrimination. This piece of legislation was insufficient for the Democrats. We wanted to amend this act to expand it even further towards our skewed ideas of equity. With Senate Bill 4 of 2023, we introduced a clause including protecting "sexual orientation" based on "gender identity or expression" to the already existing statute.[51]

Legislation initially intended to protect Americans from discrimination has become a political weapon to advance our ideology of gender and sexually oriented politics.

Political enemies such as Senator Jim Runestad argued that Senate Bill 4 was unnecessary and improper. He believed that the initial legislation was enough, and that case law determined by both Michigan and the United States Supreme Courts indicated that Senate Bill 4 was redundant, excessive, and would lead to discrimination against people outside the LGBTQIA+ community.

This clause is far from redundant; it gives us the ability to control people's lives. The conservative argument to this agenda is that they believe our additions are irrelevant and that groups we seek to privilege are already sufficiently protected. In fact, that is why we included the term "expression." It's a broad term. Lovely really, because broad terms can be used to justify broad powers for the governor and unelected bureaucrats. Adding this term allows us to use the government to increase our power over the people, most importantly the children. Civil rights don't exist for the protection of the people. They exist as a tool for the government to increase its control over the people.

Reproductive Tyranny

As the governor, I generally support policies that restrict the rights of the people. However, I also recognize the political expediency that exists when framing an argument to make it appear as though government is creating a right to give to the people. I present the people with new privileges, packaged as rights, and they thank me through their vote. It's a win-win. The people of Michigan falsely feel empowered, while my power increases thanks to their misunderstanding of freedom and willingness to sacrifice their children for their personal interest.

Every successful girl-boss needs a good catchphrase, and since I never did fix the damn roads, it was time for an upgrade. My new motto is "fighting like hell" to legalize unlimited unborn baby killing, while calling it "reproductive rights," because branding is important. This makes me sound like a true defender of liberty, which could not be further from the truth. I hate when other people have freedom. I deserve the undisputed ability to reign over all Michiganders, whether they are fully grown adults or unborn children.

My tyranny knows no bounds, which enables me to deceive many Michigan women into believing I was their advocate, and that my policies supported them. Instead, I have used these women, playing into their emotions in order to empower myself.

Abortion is the woman's right to choose to take the life of her unborn child. There have been endless debates as to whether this is a legitimate right, but I believe it is fundamental for my manipulation of women. I act as if I am supporting women by giving them the license to kill, enabling them to take the life of their child without judgment.

It's not about children, it's all about women, their rights, and my power. Besides, fetuses are not actually children, they are clumps of cells that just so happen to form into a child.

Science is very important to me. Even though "Biologists from 1,058 academic institutions around the world assessed survey items on when a human's life begins and, overall, 96% (5337 out of 5577) affirmed the fertilization view" believing that life begins at conception.[52] I disagree.

I'm proud of the 240 brave biologists who stood up for women, rejecting mainstream science and paving the way for truth and reason. Four percent of biologists are willing to put facts over feelings and tell people the cold hard truth, there is only one life that matters in a pregnancy, the life of the voting age mother.

Life begins at some undefined point that will never be proven. This leaves the door open for the right to take the life of a fetus. In Michigan, Proposal 3 of 2022 reserved the constitutionally protected right to an abortion up to the point of birth, but it is limited after viability by the clause "if medically needed to protect a patient's life or physical or mental health."[53] Remember that the only patient is the mother and if she might become emotional or stressed taking care of a baby, her mental health is at risk, essentially qualifying her for an abortion at any point in the pregnancy.

Fetal viability is the capability of the child to survive outside of the mother's womb. Sure, you can regulate child murder, but not if feelings are hurt. Just trust the science until I disagree with what the science concludes. More than 95 out of 100 scientists say that a fetus is a child, but I will continue to deny it. The scientists are only welcome in the central planning party when they agree with our quest for dominance.

The women of America enjoyed the right to destroy their unborn child's life for decades, in fact the right had been the precedent for nearly as long as I have been alive! Roe v. Wade muscled its way into American legal precedent, and it stayed there for 50 years. I supported this case as it enshrined the right to have an abortion without showing interest for the well-being of an unloved fetus.

My nemesis, Donald Trump, was outspoken in his opposition to abortion. He took issue with the right to voluntarily murder the most vulnerable, appointing conservative judges to get the job done.

Having appointed three conservative justices to the Supreme Court, which jeopardized the status of Roe v Wade, Donald Trump also appointed many conservative judges to preside over courtrooms throughout the nation. Mr. Trump, as well as his judicial appointees, wanted to destroy the right that my ideological colleagues created and defended. I could not let that happen.

On June 24, 2022, the worst fears of the Democratic Party were realized when Roe v. Wade was overturned by way of the Dobbs v. Jackson Women's Health Organization decision. We created the right to abortion to attract women to our party. Allowing Republicans to put the interest of a preborn child above the convenience of a woman is intolerable.

Abortion is a foundational aspect of human rights because without the right to abortion, what rights do we have?

In order to steer the conversation, we use clever terms such as "my body, my choice," or "a woman's right to choose," and my personal favorite, "reproductive rights." Reproductive rights can be broadly interpreted, which works to the favor of Democrats such as myself, who seek to frame the narrative around pregnancy.

Fortunately, with political motives in mind, our lobby runs deep and we are a sinister bunch. We work around the clock in order to ensure scared and confused mothers can murder their children if they so choose.

The freedom destroying Dobbs decision was leaked early in 2022, which enabled Democratic operatives to immediately work on enshrining child sacrifice into the state constitution. Referring to abortion as child sacrifice may be hard for some to digest, but that's exactly what it is, sacrificing life without their consent for the convenience of their mother.

In January 2022, the ballot committee, Reproductive Freedom for All, was formed just six months before the Dobbs decision with the sole purpose of amending the Michigan Constitution to create a permanent right for "reproductive freedom." Reproductive Freedom for All, an ironically named organization, set out to collect the signatures necessary to add abortion on demand to the 2022 general election.

Once on the ballot, the fate of the unborn was in the hands of the voters. I made sure I did everything within my power to manipulate the public into voting against preborn children. With the help of Planned Parenthood and sympathetic judges, I was able to boost the efforts in elevating a woman's ability to choose convenience over life itself.

In April 2022, Planned Parenthood filed a lawsuit against the Attorney General in the Court of Claims to ensure the 1931 abortion law protecting the unborn from the violent act of abortion would not take effect in a post Roe world. This was mere procedure as Attorney General Dana Nessel is a committed abortion accomplice.

A month later, a judge issued an injunction to temporarily block the 1931 law. This was a major victory; the 1931 law made no consideration for reproductive freedom. The draconian law cared more about life than women's rights. The 1931 law only permitted abortion in cases where the mother's life was threatened, erroneously prioritizing the life of both the child and the mother.

I can't believe how backwards society used to be. They didn't understand the political gains of devaluing life, playing into women's emotions, and driving a wedge in the sacred relationship between mother and child. Breaking the mother and child bond erodes the family unit, degrades the nuclear family, and directs society toward the government as their source of love and affection.

Although I was proud of the Attorney General for standing against life, I wasn't about to sit on the sidelines as women's convenience was under attack. For my part in the plot to prioritize abortion access over the lives of children, I filed a suit in the Oakland County Circuit Court to prevent county prosecutors from enforcing the 1931 law. I made the case that the equal protection clause and due process in Michigan's constitution, derived from the 14th Amendment, invalidated the archaic law that showed interest for both the mother and child. I then asked the Michigan Supreme Court to certify the constitutional questions involved in the case I filed at the Oakland County Circuit Court. Being a leader in the fight against babies is one of my most proud accomplishments.

The proper role of government is to protect our politician given rights. The constitution should be discarded anytime I disagree with it and is only valuable when it gives me power to control circumstances. America's Founding Fathers warned of tyrants, but the constitution is a living and breathing document meant to mold and conform with political landscapes. The opinions of these old white men have become irrelevant.

Fortunately, the Oakland County judge sided with me, issuing a temporary restraining order against the enforcement of the 1931 law. Judicial activists had set the foundation by eroding the archaic life-protecting law because it only explicitly showed interest in the mother and didn't clearly depict interest for the preborn child. We took advantage of the situation and raised the state's interest of the mother above that of the preborn child.

With the unprecedented leak of the Dobbs case and injunction of the archaic law protecting life, our work was nearly complete. The people of Michigan were presented with a choice to listen to me and denounce the sanctity of human life in the womb or be seen as a traitor and a woman hater.

Proposal 3 was a ballot initiative that sought to defy the Supreme Court decision and maintain abortion on demand in Michigan. My Democratic colleagues and I branded Prop 3 as a "fundamental right" for "reproductive freedom," and seamlessly tied it to my now famous "fight like hell" catchphrase. With millions of dollars pouring in from out of state to deceive the people of Michigan, this amendment by petition was sure to help sway hearts and minds in our direction.

When women in Michigan trust me to decide what their fundamental rights and freedoms are, I have the power to mold Michigan into what I want it to be, a progressive regime firmly under my dictatorship. Prop 3 is full of progressive changes, which the people of Michigan need whether they like it or not. The biggest recurring theme of Prop 3 is taking the parents out of the equation.

I pretend your kids have power, but truly the state fills the void left by disenfranchised parents. Prop 3 enables children to have an abortion or mutilate their body parts without the consent or even knowledge of their parents[54]. A few fundamental rights I believe minors should have extends to: abortions, sex changes, contraceptives, any form of lawful and consensual sexual activity, and an overall idea of reproductive freedom regardless of how parents think or feel.

Parents don't know what's best for their children, I do. Just like the right to steal from a bank or rob a gas station at gunpoint, killing babies is a form of freedom. Kids needed this new right to abortion and I needed to protect children from snooping parents. Prop 3 accomplishes this remarkably well. This proposal was intended to bring sweeping changes and to destroy past laws on abortion. Prop 3 is the new precedent, and it brings a new understanding of rights that I hope will triumph forever.

Proposal 3 was carefully written to target children without mentioning them. The word 'individuals' was used to subtly open the door to extreme abortion policy regardless of age. Prop 3 is a great victory for my central planning regime. By defining new rights and freedoms for all, we were able to drive a wedge between parents and children.

What I won't tell the people is how abortion comes with consequences. Enabling the right to choose to take the life of an infant does not produce mental health issues. An outdated study from 2011 published in the British Journal of Psychiatry says, "Results indicate quite consistently that abortion is associated with moderate to highly increased risks of psychological problems subsequent to the procedure."[55] The study found that women who had an abortion experienced an 81 percent increased risk for mental health issues. No woman in history has ever regretted having an abortion, at least not in America where we love freedom. Additionally, this study was a small sample size. Only 877 thousand women were analyzed, which doesn't give a sufficient representation and leaves for a high margin of error.

When there is an issue that sparks controversy amongst Michiganders, I do not attempt to use reason to honestly persuade people to join my side. I do not extend a friendly hand to those I disagree with. Instead, I used the leak of the Dobbs decision as grounds to begin immediately working to protect feticide in Michigan. Prop 3 had to be worded as broadly as possible so that parents would be rendered helpless and children would be vulnerable to the state. Motherhood is a sacred role. This is something I should know, but politically I act as if I do not. I place the child's life in the hands of the mother and her abortion doctor.

My favorite broad term is that the abortion can be done if the mother's "mental health" is affected. This was perhaps the most deceptive work yet, as mental health is open to however a health professional interprets it. Any negative emotion could check the mental health box, which allows the state to provide you the opportunity to take the life of your unborn child through all 40 weeks of pregnancy. This is your right thanks to sick humans such as myself who deceived Michigan into supporting such an extreme measure.

Living under an abortionist regime is not easy for those who oppose us. This is because they foolishly cling to the old understanding of rights, the iteration that was oppressive to women by forcing them to have children and nurture life at all stages of development. These types of people must not challenge my planning prowess. I helped to game the system by pushing reproductive tyranny on the people of Michigan.

As governor, I can trample on any rights I disagree with. Freedom of religion and freedom of speech only drag down my progressive regime. Therefore, I am open to planning a more aggressive society, one that takes care of these anti-reproductive freedom advocates. I support the type of culture in America where abortion protestors are at least ridiculed and ideally thrown in prison for lengthy sentences.

A Catholic group of ten wicked individuals recently protested outside an abortion clinic where a baby killer proudly defended the high volume of abortions he has completed. These dangerous felons were sentenced to a total of 23 years in prison for their hateful opposition to women.[56] An average of just over two years of prison for people who oppose abortion sounds necessary for a healthy and free society.

Maybe that's what I need to bring to Michigan. One of the elderly criminals, Paulette Harlow, suffers from many health conditions including diabetes, Hashimoto's Disease, and chronic back pain.[57] A prison sentence would gravely endanger her life. That danger doesn't compare to the mental health of the abortion clinic employees and their patients who were triggered by her hateful stance in support of life. What if they felt any discomfort because of the presence of the protestors? It's a good thing our judicial system with judges like Colleen Kollar- Kotelly, who much like the Oakland County judge, ruled in favor of reproductive tyranny.

Mrs. Harlow's husband begged the judge to show mercy to his sick wife. Judge Kollar-Kotelly mocked Mrs. Harlow, responding that she should "make an effort to remain alive" which she attributed to a "tenet of her religion."[58] Judge Kollar-Kotelly has a long history of helping the progressive cause from the bench, such as her block of President Trump's 2017 transgender military ban. She also presided over ACLU v. Donald Trump, a case regarding election security.

Reproductive tyranny is just one form of tyranny that people such as the judge and myself want to bring to this country. I support harsh penalties for anti-choice groups, but I believe that "peaceful" protestors should walk free. Aiding and abetting criminals while they burn down businesses is completely justifiable under our rule. This is a further example of my tyrannical hypocrisy and my willingness to punish the people of Michigan and America to strengthen our power.

Roe v. Wade was a departure from the original American understanding of rights. It was one that I welcomed, as Roe v. Wade brought to life the progressive dream of a woman's right to choose to take the life of her unborn child. The United States was founded on certain inalienable rights, including the right to life, liberty, and the pursuit of happiness. The 14th Amendment was passed to clearly specify due process and equal protection under the law. This amendment was a legal protection of the rights of all Americans. Of course, the understanding of which was rooted in the Founder's conception of rights. Roe v. Wade clearly violated the original intent of natural rights as well as the 14th Amendment.

This could not have happened soon enough. How else could the administrative state deal with overpopulation if those pesky natural rights were allowed to exist? The 14th Amendment itself was ripe for weaponization by the insertion of our clever interpretation. The penumbras that emanated from between the lines of the amendment were all that was needed to first protect marital privacy through the Griswold v. Connecticut decision and then to extend that right to killing babies under Roe v. Wade.

What was supposed to be a legal protective mechanism for Americans became a tool for judicial activism under the guise of liberty. Who shouldn't be allowed to exercise their right to privacy even if it includes killing a baby? What a fine weapon for brilliant central planners such as myself to have at our disposal!

Constitutions were not meant to be permanent. I do not believe in a fixed law of nature. I believe in the laws of Gretchen that fall in line with new age progressive thought that can be changed to whatever we want them to be. Living in a world of delusion is if nothing else entertaining, but when people such as myself hold important offices such as the governorship of Michigan, we get to impose these delusions on all of the people. We use the system to determine what should and should not be. We deceive the people into believing new freedoms exist, and upon securing their vote, I continue on my tyrannical ways while Michigan's unborn children and their parents continue to suffer because of my framed argument regarding "reproductive freedom."

Democrat, progressive, liberal, elitist, you can call me whatever you want. In practice I am just a tyrant who believes in central planning, not liberty. I seek to expand my powers, constitution be damned. I believe that rights are not inalienable, that they are not found in nature, and that they are not God-given. Freedom is the privilege I extend to those who I favor. I can create rights, and I can just as easily take them away. I am keen on taking rights away from law- abiding Michiganders and protecting the rights of criminals. I also believe in expanding privacy and the right to convenience over the right to life.

My idea of reproductive freedom reduces human life to a mere choice. The mother can choose to kill her own child if she so pleases, and it all depends on her mental health. But, don't blame the mother first. I am the one who fought hard to give her that choice.

Pregnancy used to be celebrated. Having a child marked a change in the lives of everyone within a family. It was a happy occasion. Now, under my rule, keeping a pregnancy is nothing more than a decision. If having a baby seems too troublesome, my abortionists will gladly take care of that. You can thank me for reducing the miracle of life into another arbitrary daily choice.

My reasoning was simple; aborted babies don't vote. In this country we still act like the people's voice matters. I need votes to keep my grip on power. Selling "reproductive freedom" to women helps them feel empowered and comfortable as they virtue signal over the silliest things in life instead of valuing their own children. I value convenience over human life and votes over people. I solidified the right of women to choose to take the life of their unborn child because it is politically expedient to secure the demented feminist vote rather than fight on behalf of the vulnerable.

Environmental Injustice

I love instilling fear where people otherwise live peaceful lives, ruling by emergency decree. Panic is needed in order to consolidate my control over the people. I vowed that Michigan would adopt an aggressive partisan agenda to transition the state's energy policy towards the unproven, expensive promises of "clean" energy.

This is yet another example of my willingness to sell out Michigan to the ideological agenda of my progressive party. A bipartisan bill passed in 2016 which established a 15 percent renewable energy standard. Fifteen percent is not enough for me or those who bankroll my campaign. In less than 20 years, Michigan is set to be entirely "green." The state is expected to jump from its current level of 12 percent up to 60 percent in a decade.[59] The numbers are astronomical and impractical. That doesn't matter, I care about making my colleagues happy. That's how I continue my career ambitions. I don't answer to Michigan, I answer to corporate elitists and special interest groups. I answer to donors and the Green New Deal. The progress of my career is far more important than the well-being of everyday lives. Donors and bureaucrats want clean energy, so I force it on the people of Michigan.

Environmentalism leaves behind Michigan farmers. This is not a gross oversight, even though Michigan's farmers help feed both the people of Michigan and the country. I claimed to support the empowerment of essential workers during my lockdowns, but this was sabotage. I do not care about those who truly provide essential services, like farmers.

Fertilizer prices have shot up, and I have no intention of helping small farmers. As a result, new acreage of wheat and corn significantly declined in 2022. In 2023, fertilizer accounted for 45 percent of farmer's costs.[60] Loren Koeman, lead economist at the Farm Bureau, described the reality for Michigan's farmers stating, "We saw huge run-ups with peaks in that 2022 to 2023 time frame where prices went up four to five times. We've somewhat settled back down, but prices are about double what they historically have been, back in 2018 or 2019."[61] My regime has made it harder for farmers to do their jobs. They feel a real financial pinch, but that's by design.

My administration does not want small, independent farmers. They pose too great of a risk to my agenda. I would rather invite large corporations who sponsor globalist policies into Michigan than aid farmers who have lived here for generations. Keeping prices high discourages farmers from independent operation, allowing me to use the bureaucracy to usher in alternative energy and globalism.

My bureaucracy does not prioritize the needs of Michigan farmers. Foreigners own a sizable chunk of Michigan's land, which includes farmland. A grand total of 1.35 million Michigan acres are owned by foreign investors.[62] The appreciating value of farmland could attract further foreign ownership of Michigan land, taking independence away from farmers at home and giving it to faraway financiers. Increased farm real estate[63] could also attract foreign investments from China, who already has established a policy of buying farmland throughout the United States. I'm sure that our Healthy Michigan Plan will help convince my partners in the Chinese Communist Party to take land ownership away from hard- working Michigan farmers.

Foreigners are not the only eager investors in Michigan agriculture. The ever philanthropic Bill Gates has been so kind as to invest in my state. I appreciate "Farmer Bill's" commitment to spreading globalist policies to Michiganders. Farmer Bill owns more farmland in America than anyone else, putting him in a prime position to control our nation's food supply.[64] Who better to own so much tillable farmland than someone who believes in population control and pushes synthetic meats as well as other alternative food sources?

There is no harm in having a globalist so involved in the food supply. While Mr. Gates does advocate for lab-made "meat" compounds, surely he would not have a nefarious motive for buying so much farmland to advance his product. Although Michigan farms have provided families with authentic food, this must change. Just like the rest of the small businesses in Michigan, these little farms are not greasing my manicured palms. Farmer Bill agrees that we need environmental injustice.

Mr. Gates supports bureaucracies such as mine that enact the globalist policies he sponsors. Michiganders don't need their own land, and they don't need their own food. Farmer Bill and I see the big picture, that experts should rule. We are smarter than you, so we will sell you out to large corporations as well as for billionaire pet projects, such as Mr. Gates' impossible meat or the vaccines that he pushes across the world.

It takes a large bureaucracy to enact central planning policies. My appointed bureaucrats need to be loyal to me, not to the people of Michigan, or any sense of freedom or natural rights. They should only recognize one boss, me, the one who appointed them to their well-paid positions. I reorganized the Department of Environmental Quality into the Department of Environment, Great Lakes, and Energy (EGLE) and immediately expanded this department. But I wasn't done yet; I pulled a classic move from the progressive playbook in unconstitutional governance.

Through executive order, I authorized EGLE to form a commission that would centrally plan climate change response. Expanding the bureaucratic web by adding this 23 person commission filled with experts was critical. Executive orders are my favorite way to govern. Sometimes I wonder why the legislature exists at all, but then I remember that many of them do support me and I can use them to my advantage. Oftentimes I work with them to create new commissions and to give me more power. And if we're being honest, the appearance of "separation of powers" helps make my tyrannical reign more palatable to my more moderate Democrat and Republican subjects.

This commission on climate change knows they answer to me. Their job is to advise EGLE and myself on policy objectives they believe I support. I let them know when they are wrong. Coming up with my own set of facts and fabricating a narrative is what I do best.

I use my familiar ways of deception and fear-mongering to explain my expansion of the government to my subjects. The first line of the executive order reads, "The science is clear, and message urgent."[65] The urgency is to instill fear within the people describing how inaction is the greatest problem facing Michigan's future.

The science told everyone to hunker down inside their homes to avoid the virus. However, the science now demands that everyone rally to support my bureaucratic program of regulations, or else we will be wiped out by environmental disaster. I am not in the business of weather forecasting, I am into broadcasting fear. Using my science, I warn the people that an emergency is imminent. Emergencies are my time to shine, setting aside my favorite pleather blazer and hot fuschia lipstick, and grabbing my executive order signing pen to give myself more power.

I need fear to compel people into complying with my unconstitutional regulations and mandates. While I expand governmental powers, I fill your minds with fear in order to manipulate you into believing that my consolidation of power is necessary.

EGLE, as well as the commission that was entirely obedient to me, were tasked with forming a plan for environmental policy in Michigan. The commission produced a 58 page report detailing the priorities of centrally planned environmental policy. To instill fear, my cronies linked climate change to the everyday lives of Michiganders. The message was clear; if our plan was not adopted, then life would get worse for those already struggling, and it would become bad for those who lived peaceful, quiet lives. This was projection, as it would actually be the Healthy Climate Plan that made life worse overall for every citizen.

Michigan has been the proud home to many different types of farmers for centuries. I take issue with this. These farmers are too loyal to the soil. They value their families, and they value the farms passed down to them from generation to generation. Their commitment to producing food for others as well as living on their own is rather selfish. They don't embrace the science of my central planning. They don't allow themselves to feel the fear that I so desperately spread.

Take the Johnson family, cherry farmers from the Traverse City region, for example. I have claimed that climate change is what has caused their poor yields. Higher temperatures disrupt seasonal cycles, therefore it is climate change that has ruined their yields in years past, and it will only get worse.

The Johnsons refuse to trust the science. They claim that the reason for their lower yield is because they were coerced into reducing how much costly fertilizer they spread on their farm. What fools! Clearly that has nothing to do with their crop yield and they are small, weak, and incompetent failing farmers.

They seem to believe that nature can't be controlled the way I say it can. What little faith they have; my climate change policies directly address their issue. As the plan states, "Climate change increases the likelihood of natural disasters, damaging infrastructure that is costly to repair and disrupts business. More erratic and unpredictable temperatures lead to uncertainty and losses for our farmers and other sectors that rely on seasonal consistency."[66]

Follow the guidelines, or else natural disasters will suddenly appear and destroy both crops and infrastructure. Follow the guidelines, or else we guarantee that every single year will be hotter and more unpredictable than the last, ruining the family farm forever. It's funny how even environmental bureaucracy can relate to my slogan, "fix the damn roads." Though it might seem that the roads can be repaired despite slightly warmer temperatures than in past years, my team of advisors found a way to link infrastructure to climate change. This is the science that the public has to accept as truth.

One of the stated goals of the Michigan Healthy Climate Plan is to guarantee the "abundance" and "health" of Michigan's land and resources. The plan can't legitimately guarantee either promise. In fact, the plan makes it harder to have abundant, healthy land, especially for farmers.

Climate change planning includes the expansion of wind and solar power. The stated goal is to reduce carbon emissions. Of course, relying on trees to do so makes too much sense, so my bureaucracy is aimed at transitioning all of Michigan's energy sources towards what we have deemed to be "clean." Installing solar panels and windmills is highly disruptive. It takes away rural, open land that otherwise would have been used by farmers. Instead of raising crops or livestock, there will be giant metal structures transforming Michigan's beautiful, quiet landscapes into ugly industrial zones. This reduces the amount of total land available for farmers, and takes away the services they provide, such as feeding the state and the nation.

The damage done by science to the farmers is harsh enough, but the plan does not stop there. The numbers indicate that Michiganders are struggling. This is odd, because the employment numbers that President Biden loves to tout indicate that everyone is working and making a living for themselves. The Michigan Healthy Climate Plan highlighted a more disturbing reality, "It shows that even with unemployment at record low levels, much of our population struggles to make ends meet." The plan cites 38 percent of Michiganders struggling. Over one-third of the state is having a hard time surviving day by day. Officially 13 percent are below the poverty line, and the other 25 percent are not far from it. Clearly, the best course of action for our struggling neighbors is more government intervention. They need to be aware that bureaucracy will save them from climate change, even though the same bureaucracy could not, and would not, save them from the hard economic situation the government imposed on the people.

This scientific, progressive plan would not be complete without obligatory inclusion of equity. The Healthy Climate Plan brings with it claims towards environmental justice. This is supposed to sound like a noble ideal, but it's not. It's deception. Environmental justice entails picking winners and losers. The plan describes my heavy involvement within this section of the program, "Gov. Whitmer called on those developing the MI Healthy Climate Plan to design and recommend decarbonization strategies that will prioritize and advance equity and environmental justice." Advancing equity is my way of choosing who my bureaucracy decides to financially support.

If nothing is done, "Climate change will only deepen these existing harms and inequities."[67] Including racial equity within the plan allows me to leverage this policy as a political piece. If life is already hard for a person who belongs to a group I have recognized as disadvantaged, I promote policies such as climate planning as a means of promising that their life will improve. It won't, but I appreciate their votes. It's not "climate change" that will worsen harm, but my reign.

Mussel Lives Matter

Attorney General Dana Nessel took the lead on punishing Lee Mueller and his business, Boyce Hydro, which has operated many local dams. Mr. Mueller's crime wasn't a simple accident. His unforgivable offense to my green regime was the fact that "thousands if not millions"[68] of freshwater mussels lost their lives because of his damn dam breaking.

I could have forgiven damage to property, and maybe even the death of citizens. But freshwater mussels? No, this damage is unforgivable.

Fortunately, a fellow progressive like Dana Nessel was there fighting diligently for the rights of freshwater mussels from the beginning. My regime warmly welcomes mussels, Bill Gates, solar "snake oil" salesmen, abortionists, and anyone obedient to my orders. My regime is hostile to those who have the audacity to believe that they can live without my expertise. That includes business owners, such as Mr. Mueller.

In October 2018, Boyce Hydro opened a few of its gates as a precautionary measure for winter. They claimed they did this for the safety of their workers and the community at large as well as for the survival of the dam itself. A year later, the company requested permission from EGLE to lower the water level again for the safety of the community. Clearly, the owner knew his dam was getting weaker.

The company told us this, claiming that the Edenville dam could not likely meet half of the flood requirement. We had no advice for them but to figure it out, or be punished. In November 2019, Boyce Hydro had the audacity to lower the levels upon their own independent assessment, similar to what they had done the year prior. Mr. Mueller claimed higher water levels could cause a dam break but he wasn't thinking about the well-being of mussels. Don't they know these types of decisions are reserved to me and my bureaucrat buddies? Mussels lived there and mussel lives matter!

Well, they sure know now and hopefully learned their lesson. Dana Nessel made them pay 120 million dollars per the court decision siding with my central planning pals. Lee Mueller stated, "The state agencies clearly care more about mussels living in the impoundment than they do about the people living downstream of the dams."[69] While this is true, Mr. Mueller clearly intended to criticize our authority with his comment. This is why Attorney General Nessel had to punish him for being a bigot against mussels.

Nessel described our mission to, "Vindicate the rights of the public to enjoy and benefit from MI natural resources, including the freshwater mussels."[70] The mussels have rights. A Michigan citizen owning and operating his own business does not have rights, and should not question why we believe mussels are more important than people.

EGLE knew. Dana Nessel knew. Yet whenever Boyce Hydro would attempt to cooperate with the government, we would either not respond or demand they take action at odd times. Boyce claims it made its decisions based on the safety of its workers and the people downstream.

What about the safety of the mussels? EGLE and Attorney General Nessel fought for the mussels, and unfortunately the dam broke as a result. It was clearly the fault of Boyce Hydro. Defending the Attorney General I said, "There is a lot of information out there that is not exactly accurate, one of which is the assumption that it was the state that said to raise the level."[71] Anyone blaming the state is clearly spreading misinformation. It's not like we continually told them to raise it while knowing the dam's structural integrity was not sound. We use the two-tiered justice system to exonerate ourselves of any wrongdoing, because we fought the good fight to give Michigan mussels a healthy home.

Mr. Mueller was left with a hefty fee to clean up the damages that we caused. That's justice in a bureaucratic regime. The private individual or company is always at fault, usually because they did not blindly obey our orders. The people should know that we know what is best, and private entities only obstruct our environmental central planning.

Grade A Control

The work done by the state of Michigan to cover up our involvement in the dam breaks was unparalleled. Break the damn dams doesn't have as nice of a ring to it as "fix the damn roads."

Similarly, the effectiveness of my administration speaks for itself. I approved of the Michigan Healthy Climate Plan, and my commission of experts all agreed that the science confirmed the genius of our policy. I did not need approval from the people or from the legislature. Their support is expected, but far from necessary for my rule. Bureaucracy and executive power is the way to bring science and democracy to the people of Michigan, whether they like it or not.

It came as an unwelcome surprise when the Mackinac Center for Public Policy issued a report card for my environmental planning policies, and they gave me failing grades. The report card evaluated the alternative, clean sources of energy advocated by my bureaucracy.[72] The report card boasted one well deserved A as my brilliant planning is deserving of the highest praises. That A grade came in carbon sequestration, the primary stated objective of the Michigan Healthy Climate Plan. However, the Mackinac Center somehow stated that the reason for the high grade was because of Michigan's forests, which comprise around half of the state's total land mass. How dare they attribute this clean energy to an actual scientific fact found in nature. I could have easily used this as a political talking point to fool the public into believing that my policies were the reason Michigan fared well in emission reduction.

They then had the audacity to assign four consecutive failing grades in the categories of solar, hydroelectric, geothermal, and wind based energies. They insinuate that relying on solar energy is bad policy. That can't be, I have staked a large part of Michigan's future on solar energy. Apparently, solar energy works in the regions with the most sunlight, such as in the Southwest. Michigan is a very cloudy state, seeing approximately 60 days of sunny conditions per year. I'm sure those 60 days are more than enough to power the electric grid for 10 million people.

In terms of hydroelectric energy, Michigan is sure to succeed due to the abundance of water. However, rivers and mountains are the main source of hydropower. Michigan is flat, and what we have in lakes we lack in rivers. Wind-powered energy is definitely smart policy. The bitter cold of Michigan winters makes it feel like the winds are stronger than is reality. Despite Michigan only having average wind output, any logical person should concede power generation is driven by perceived levels of wind, not actual wind levels.

The metrics that promise wind-power as a true alternative are based on optimal conditions. Forecasting based on optimal conditions is a reliable way to plan for the future and sets the foundation for blaming climate change when things go unexpectedly wrong.

The Greatest Gift

Giving the best gifts isn't easy. The price tag isn't everything when it comes to handing over a special prize for someone you care deeply about; oftentimes it takes a lot of work. Fortunately, Michigan has a strong team ready to accomplish the unthinkable.

Power hungry men from around the nation poured tens of millions of dollars into making Michigan a playground for the global elite. I knew they were relying on me to lead the effort to undermine the will of the people, placing a lot on my shoulders.

For the first time in 40 years, we did it! Using every trick in the book, Democrats successfully usurped power from the people.

At noon on January 1st, 2023, the keys to my kingdom were handed to me when the Michigan House and Senate flipped from Republican control to Democratic control, giving me ultimate power.

By the grace of elitists, I've been chosen as the shiny, girl-boss pawn for the powerful elite. I'm no longer simply aiming to please my daddy. Having bigger fish to fry, billionaires to impress, and prospective investors to win over, my sights are on sitting in the Oval Office.

Early in 2023, it became clear we had a major problem in Lansing. With 56 Democrats and 54 Republicans in the state house, we have a narrow majority. When a big project is ready to come to Michigan, my team needs to be united to ensure the central planning comes to fruition or else relying on Republicans is in order.

A freshman state representative named Dylan Wegela, a self-proclaimed Democratic Socialist from Inkster, came to Lansing with a mind of his own. Blown away by his sincerity and convictions, my team was left stunned. It was like the guy actually believes what we sell to the voters every election season! Unfortunately for this naive young socialist, our fragile majority was bought and paid for by elites, and the actual voters are the least of their concerns. If he wants to play ball, he'll have to learn to grease the right wheels.

Big donors and special interest groups had made it clear to me what they wanted, but this guy just didn't want to help them. He made claims like "poor people aren't getting a special handout, why should this large corporation?"

Representative Wegela's foolishness would be laughable if not for the fact that he could have cost me my political career.

The First Gift

Knowing we had a problem on our hands in Representative Wegela, my team and I understood the assignment; flip a few weak-kneed Republicans and make our wildly unpopular bills bipartisan. Inevitably a few Republicans join ranks with Democrats at crucial times in return for deals made behind closed doors.

On January 26th, 2023, with 24 votes in the Senate and 60 votes in the House, Senate Bill 7 was the first major financial test of the 102nd Legislature and we won! Appropriating over one billion dollars for numerous projects, most notably 200 million dollars to revitalize a paper mill in the upper peninsula, was a massive victory for my friends.

In an effort to show strong bipartisan support, some of the more courageous Republicans started talking with their colleagues to drum up more support for this gift. One member even went so far as to promise another member whatever he wanted in return for a vote for this special handout. It's a shame that some legislators are too inexperienced and ineffective to realize that selling out to the elitists is a sure way to become powerful.

Some people wonder why hundreds of millions of taxpayer dollars are used to bail out private companies; these people simply don't understand freedom. As elected officials, we are free to take the people's money and use it for whatever purposes we want. That's the American Dream.

Knowing 60 out of 110 members of the House, 24 out of 38 members of the Senate, and the best central planner our state has ever seen, me of course, had the power to give 200 million dollars of taxpayer money to one private company is something I'll always cherish.

Equal opportunity and equal protection under the law is a main tenet of the US Constitution.[73] However, Michigan's Constitution provides a special opportunity to take money from the people to give to politicians' friends who fund their re-election efforts.

Article 4, Section 30 of the Michigan Constitution says we can steal money from the people to be used for private purposes if two-thirds of both chambers of the legislature and the governor agree to the plan.[74]

Although some quick math reveals neither 60 out of 110 nor 24 out of 38 meets the two-thirds threshold. Who really cares? Any Michigander who would complain about a technicality like this is bigoted against special interests.

Far right extremists will say the Michigan Constitution and laws that are passed are supposed to fall within the bounds of the United States Constitution for the purpose of protecting the rights of the people.[75] Oftentimes they will even claim rights are God-given and don't come from the government. These idiots clearly haven't read the Michigan Constitution which proves the government can do what we want with citizens' tax dollars!

In the bigger picture, 200 million dollars isn't that much money, especially when ten million people in the state of Michigan each pay their fair share to help causes supported by the government. On average, 20 dollars from every man, woman, and child is next to nothing. One hundred dollars taken from a family of five isn't going to impact their well-being, especially when they are used to it. We in government support these projects all the time with the people's money. Maybe one day if you become the CEO of a big corporation, hire a lobbyist to advocate for your special interest, and donate big sums of money to my campaign, I'll take money from taxpayers to help your company as well.

We all know my friend, Mark Zuckerberg, could have funded the project himself when he was only 23, but he's been more focused on influencing our elections. That's why he gave grants to 2,500 local municipalities across the nation to install drop boxes[76] which are proven to be the most secure way of voting in our nation's history.

The Second Gift

Years ago, Republicans in Michigan created a scenario that once a certain revenue threshold for the state's general fund was eclipsed, it would automatically trigger a reduction in the personal income tax from 4.25 percent to 4.05 percent.[77] This short-sighted decision to leave more money in the pockets of the hardworking middle class inevitably meant less money for the government to spend. How stupid can government officials be to reduce the amount of funds we get to control? Letting foolish people invest money as they see fit instead of how we see fit is one of the dumbest ideas imaginable and goes directly against the concepts of central planning. Fortunately, the attorney general stepped in to ensure the uniform tax cut didn't last more than one year.[78]

Getting what I want is easy when I have the right people in leadership positions in the legislature. Senate Majority Leader Winnie

Brinks loves corporate welfare and handing out special favors to big donors and special interest groups. She has a 100 percent scorecard rating from the Mackinac Center for Public Policy on business subsidy support, meaning when it's time for the government to pick winners and losers by taking from the poor and giving to our rich friends, I can count on her help. Sure, the vast majority of elected officials can be counted on to deliver crony handouts, but there's only one who tops the charts, and Winnie is that winner with over 7.5 billion dollars that she's voted to steal from you and to give to her friends.[79]

Given that ten million people live in Michigan, it is easy to rob from the poor to give to the rich. It's not like we have to take a lot of money from any one individual. During Winnie's time in office, she has voted to take 750 dollars from every man, woman, and child to give to her friends. This type of gifting is admirable. From each hard-working middle class citizen according to his ability to each crony capitalist according to his wants; that's my motto and Winnie agrees. It's not like a family of five would be better off with an extra 3,750 dollars in their pockets!

Joe Tate is far less experienced than seasoned politician Winnie Brinks. After my global elite friends and I catapulted Democrats into the majority in the state house, Joe Tate was launched into the power seat as he became the Speaker of the House. Just like I am a pawn for the global elite interests, Speaker Tate is my pawn. The Lansing lobbyists and I control him much more than he realizes. Don't get me wrong, he's a good guy, he's just in over his head.

Having mastered the trick of doing what special interest groups want in order to move up the ranks in politics, Speaker Tate is no dummy, he's just not cut out for politics like I am. After all, taking marching orders from people in Lansing who want special deals isn't all that complicated, but navigating the field of other legislators looking to do the same thing does have its complexities.

A little known fact is the role lobbyists play in picking the next Speaker of the House. Presumably the Republicans were going to hold a majority in the house, so Lansing insiders were pushing most of their money toward Republican leadership to distribute money to Republican campaigns around the state. Unfortunately for them, my friends from outside the state poured so much money into Michigan to influence the election, and the Lansing machine was unmatched.

With how far left the Democratic Party has gone in recent years, the special interest groups would have preferred balanced power, but the global elitists spoke with the money they pumped into my campaign, as well as the money they put into the ballot proposals. The people of Michigan had no chance to see through the smoke and mirror scheme of our deceptive tactics. Now Michigan belongs to me. My voter base wants far- left policies and my donors want corporate elitism. Naturally, I have chosen to deliver on both fronts.

On February 9th, 2023, the State of Michigan was in for a real treat. For those who like fireworks, rich treats, and favoritism, I wasn't about to disappoint. With Valentine's Day right around the corner, I was ready to show the people of Michigan just how much I love spending their money for them.

My team came up with a clever way to inject half a billion dollars for my friends into a series of individual bills that had previously been voted on and when consolidated became House Bill 4001. Earlier in the year, several Republicans in the house had voted on portions of this compiled bill, putting them into a difficult spot. The old bait and switch; pretty sneaky, I know.

Successfully carrying the most corrupt policies across the finish line has proven to be more difficult than I imagined with Representative Wegela standing on principle over getting things done for elitists. He showed his unreasonableness with Senate Bill 7, but House Bill 4001 would prove to bring forward substantial complexities for which none of us could have been fully prepared.

Backroom deals and trading votes are straightforward tactics that work with most politicians. Unfortunately, a rare few make political favors difficult by voting against my agenda, or worse, exposing our ways to the public. This is why I hired former state senator, operative Curtis Hertel, to twist arms when needed.

Representative Wegela tried to hide from my team and was quite successful in the days leading up to the vote. Once session started and the representatives convened, the tables were turned and the games began.

Curtis Hertel's job isn't to educate members on the bills before them, it's not even to advocate that the members vote in support of them. Mr. Hertel has one job, it's to compel members to vote for policies I support, and I expect him to deliver. He knows that and he's my man for the job.

Early that afternoon Curtis summoned Representative Wegela to the backroom and offered him a special deal. Knowing Representative Wegela represents Inkster, where the government school system had collapsed and is a touchy subject for their community, my team had the brilliant idea to trade him 40 million dollars to bail out the failed school district in return for his vote in support of House Bill 4001. Curtis and the team pitched this to Representative Wegela but after nearly 30 minutes of attempting to convince him to make this decision, he said no deal.

Meanwhile, Speaker Tate was trying to work over a Republican knowing we either needed every Democrat to vote yes or at least one Republican if we couldn't get Representative Wegela. Irritatingly, our plan was not coming to fruition so House leadership invoked Rule 32.

Rule 32 means that members are expected to sit in their assigned seats. When there's only a few votes on the agenda, which occurs most of the time, activity is more laid back and members are given latitude to move about as they see fit, mingling with colleagues about bills and other legislative work. Rule 32 is typically only used when there is a lot on the agenda and leadership wants to quickly get through voting.

In this circumstance, we had a problem and my team knew it. When things get chaotic, it's important for those in power to control the situation. Members moving about talking with one another about the failing process to get the votes wasn't going to help us complete this task. Members sitting in their seats, doing what they are told and not asking questions however, is a power play at our disposal and it was deployed.

The nice thing about Rule 32 is leadership can exempt certain members from the rule. Speaker Tate knew the mission and gave latitude to Representative Wegela to leave his seat. Not because we were happy with him but because it was time to apply more pressure.

A straightforward deal was no longer the plan; Curtis Hertel and the team came up with a new deal for Representative Wegela. His options now were to commit to voting yes on the bill, or Lansing insiders would start calling his community leaders to notify them that he was holding up money to bail out their public school system.[80]

This friendly offer put Representative Wegela in quite a quandary. Vote against his principles and get a massive gift for his community, or vote no and stay true to his convictions.

The fool just didn't get it. After another 30 minutes of twisting his arm, Curtis again was unable to negotiate a deal with the stubborn legislator. It was time to call his community leaders, and that's exactly what happened.

My team successfully turned Inkster community bigwigs against the representative who stayed true to the principles of his district. He got what he deserved; any member who is willing to put his convictions above the elitist agenda ought to be punished.

Hours continued to pass by and members continued to be subjected to their seats, except for Representative Wegela and a couple others of course. Arm twisting, back breaking, and manipulation continued as Representative Wegela was called back for a third time to meet with Mr. Hertel. It became evident that Republican support was needed for this operation given Representative Wegela's unwillingness to succumb to the pressure.

Late that evening after failing to get Representative Wegela to support a bill he was passionately opposed to, the floor leader, Representative Abraham Aiyash moved that there be a Call of the House. This motion compels each member's attendance and for the sergeant-at-arms to arrest and present absent members.

From a different back room, a member was escorted to the House floor by sergeants as HB 4001 was put on the board for a vote. While everyone else was in their seats, this other member hadn't been seen for hours, but onto the floor he came. In what amounted to nearly a straight walk, this legislator entered the House floor from one side of the chamber, visibly in tears as he pushed the green button voting yes, and continued walking without missing a step. We had done it, 56 yes votes out of 110, the exact number needed for a majority to pass this corporate elite bill!

During his downtime trying to convince Representative Wegela to vote for our crony handout, Mr. Hertel was busy strong-arming this other member to give us the vote we needed. I'm so proud of our brave team for putting Republicans in a jam to execute my global elite mission to give yet another gift to my friends.

The Greatest Gift

Electric vehicle battery plants are the new fad for decision makers and power brokers around the nation. They provide a unique dynamic in that the demand state governments have for attracting them is incredibly high, whereas the demand from consumers to purchase electric vehicles remains very low. I have used my influence in the budgetary process to ensure electric vehicle production expands. It doesn't matter that the decisions I make are at the expense of the taxpayer or that people don't want to purchase the products I'm pushing.

Using taxpayer money to accomplish my agenda is something that makes me proud of the work I do. From supporting racist budgets to supporting the Chinese Communist Party, my priorities are in order.

A little known fact about the 2023-2024 fiscal year's budget is that Section 1017 allocates 10 million dollars for minority-owned small businesses. That's right, ethnicity is a qualifier for eligibility for this program. Racism against white people is socially acceptable so I take advantage of the opportunity to pander to minorities.[81]

Being who I am, I can't help but note that this section is not exclusively about racism, it's also about taking every opportunity possible to support my Chinese Communist Party friends. I don't care about the Chinese people, I care about the Chinese Communist Party; there's a big difference. These operations aren't about caring for humanity, they are about controlling humanity. Section 1017(5)(a) of the 2023-2024 budget states: "The Department [of Labor and Economic Opportunity] shall seek to award not less than 25 percent of [the 10 million dollars] to support small businesses in alternative energy sectors, including electric vehicles. For purposes of this section, electric vehicles also include the development of Michigan-based small businesses that manufacture, deploy, or design the charging infrastructure or equipment that will support electric vehicles."[82]

I've gotten a lot of praise for this move, finding a way to simultaneously be racist and help my global elite friends to impose their electric vehicle battery operations on the State of Michigan wasn't easy, but we made it happen.

This 2.5 million dollar project amounts to only pennies per person in Michigan.[83] Unlike other asks, this price tag could be seen as insulting to my biggest supporters who expect more from the people.

Frankly, if it wasn't for the racist aspect to this take-and-spend project, it wouldn't have been worth it.

With Michigan's budget being around 80 billion dollars per year, elitists like very big rewards in return for the meals they buy legislators and the time they spend lobbying. Giving over one percent of the state budget to one private company makes for a great gift, the greatest gift of my political career.

Picking who should get the greatest gift was one of the easiest decisions of my time central planning for the State of Michigan. Contemporary Amperex Technology Co. (CATL), is a global leader in innovative technology. Having acquired cobalt from children working in the Congo for their lithium battery production, CATL is known for their forward thinking strategies and humanitarian approach to the environment and child labor opportunities. Unfortunately, anti- child advocates raised scrutiny toward this upstanding company for giving children the chance to earn a buck.[84]

Having supported piles of red tape, I understand the value of eliminating a competitor with burdensome regulations that tie up small businesses. Applying this approach to child labor however is disgraceful. Just because adults are unwilling to endure inhumane conditions for terrible wages doesn't mean they should deprive children in foreign countries from having the right to work.

In an effort to help out my global elitist friends who had this unforeseen setback from their cobalt acquisition, CATL was the clear choice to hand out the greatest gift. On March 1, 2023, House Bill 4016 was presented to the legislature for consideration. With 1.3 billion dollars designated for special programs throughout the state, the majority was earmarked for the Marshall Megasite to develop land for CATL to produce their electric vehicle batteries.[85]

Seeing our vision, the local community leadership banded together to offer a 15 year tax abatement valued at 772 million dollars for CATL, bringing the total patchwork of handouts to 1.7 billion dollars for this project funded by Michigan taxpayers.[86]

One of my favorite parts about this gift is the fact that numerous local and state officials signed non-disclosure agreements to keep this gift a secret.[87] Behind closed doors conversations about the decisions politicians make to give gifts to our friends wouldn't be nearly as effective if we didn't have assurance our efforts would be kept a secret from the people until the point of no return.

Stealing money from the people to give gifts to my friends, who promise to build things that people don't want, is one of my most noteworthy accomplishments. The greatest gifts come with big price tags for the taxpayers, and I wouldn't have it any other way.

Globalism

Speaking at the World Economic Forum is a highlight of my time as a politician. I am honored to know the global elitists have confidence in me. Showing the most powerful people in the world I am a reliable pawn for their special interests has taken a lot of work. As their agenda is global domination, precision is needed to successfully deceive the people throughout the world.

Manipulating society for globalists profits is extremely complicated and requires coordination from insiders including businessmen, politicians, and the media. With fewer questions asked and more conformity to the status quo, my friends are more successful in bringing their agenda to fruition for all of humanity. Apathy from the people and complacency from insiders is paramount for our success.

Creating an Apathetic Populace

Christianity and the nuclear family are two forces that threaten our success in the quest for global control. The growing sentiment in recent decades that people shouldn't talk about politics and religion has been paramount to bringing forward the objectives needed to take over the world. The less people know about what is actually going on, the better.

When people put their trust in the government to look after them, it places elitists in the driver's seat to make the decisions they need to steer people where they want them.

The vast majority of society doesn't trust the government, but curiously enough, they trust their own elected officials. U.S. Congress hit a record low 12 percent approval rating in February of 2024,[88] yet for some reason incumbents keep winning re-election efforts.

People trust their own congressman for two reasons, the first being the most obvious. Millions of dollars in campaign funds from special interest groups help politicians broadcast their message out to the community, deceiving the voters and earning their confidence. Secondly, the political system is corrupt and brings well-intentioned people into dark places, whether they realize it or not. I'm a prime example of that.

The more people rely on political advertisements funded by special interest groups with self-interested agendas, and the more politicians do what special interest groups want and in return receive campaign contributions, the more the system is tilted into the favor of the global elitists. This phenomenon, although not all that complicated and fairly well understood by the people, is simply too difficult to overcome in most circumstances. Their grip on society is so strong and powerful, it's almost impossible to break through.

Many well-intentioned people decide not to vote or are deceived by their incumbent because of their pleasant nature and general good intentions. If good intentions meant good actions, politics wouldn't be the same and my friends wouldn't put their trust in me to execute their agenda. The world would be a better place for billions of people, but my friends wouldn't have the control they want.

Lobbyists are essential in persuading elected officials to do what my elitist friends want. Hiring experts to convince politicians to do their bidding is cost-effective as they use the government to their advantage.

Random citizens off the street who just want the government to leave them alone are better off just accepting their fate than competing with the millions of dollars in lobby power from special interests. Trying to save a few hundred bucks a year by cutting wasteful government spending is a pathetic waste of time when their efforts pale in comparison to the influence lobbyists have over the system. The return on investment is not worth the time for everyday people.

Aside from leading a movement to challenge the system, people should understand they have two realistic options, become apathetic and accept government for what it has become, or become complacent by joining the team of using government for personal interests.

Securing Complacency

There are varying degrees of complacency. Anyone can justify their own actions if they try hard enough. I say the government creates jobs and helps manufacturing when we use the people's money to hand out gifts for privileged companies with ties to the Chinese Communist Party. Only looking at the project itself and not at all the damage done to the taxpayers helps me to feel better about my involvement and earns me trust with very powerful people who fund my campaign efforts.

Legislators oftentimes vote in support of bills they don't agree with in order to move up the ladder. Thinking about how badly they want to be the chair of a committee the following term, or their ambitions to be in a position of leadership, it is an easy justification for someone who believes they can play the game of central planning better than others.

Businessmen who want to see a profit can hardly be blamed for accepting a handout because of how difficult it is to get by in a society with burdensome regulations. Fortunately, free money isn't the only gift available for businesses. Oftentimes the government regulating their industry helps to hamstring small businesses, getting their pesky competition out of the way. Many people probably think large businesses would want to advocate against burdensome regulations and that they would use their influence to lobby the government for a more business-friendly environment. Complying with regulations is a small price to pay when their competitors close their doors; this earns complacency from corporate America.

The more people conform to status quo operations, the more power is centralized into fewer and fewer hands. Deep down inside, 99 percent of society would not only agree that there is a problem with status quo politics, but with a thorough understanding of the process would agree that things should be different. Fortunately for my powerful friends, people are trapped in apathy, complacency, or at minimum frustration because the world around them is so corrupted that there is no escaping the effects of the machine.

It's a dog-eat-dog world out there and people either take what they can from it or they leave wealth on the table for others. The problem is the masters keep the lion's share for themselves. Most people complacent with status quo operations don't even realize they are being used, they are just thinking about their own interest. Given my political aspirations, I'm not complacent with just Michigan politics; the impact caused by my quest for power has ripple effects that cause suffering throughout our nation and the entire world. That's other people's problem. My focus is on myself and my rise to power; nobody should fault me for playing the game. I'm good at what I do.

Presidential Expectations

Decades ago, it was believed that the President of the United States was expected to simply look out for the best interest of our country. Since the mid-1950s, the United States has lost the competitive advantage on manufacturing and the responsibility of our leader has shifted to a global focus.

Globalism isn't about keeping decency, order, and world peace, it's about using people throughout the world to benefit the interests of the most powerful people. More money, more material, and more power for elitists is the objective and politicians like Ronald Reagan, Ron Paul, and Donald Trump, who aren't complacent in the objective, must be shut down.

One of my personal heroes, President Richard Nixon, famous for his ability to be corrupted, destroyed the gold standard by terminating the Bretton Woods agreement and making the U.S. dollar the reserve currency of the world. With U.S. federal reserve notes essentially recognized as the new gold, America has been well equipped to take advantage of the rest of the world for our personal profits through a trade deficit scheme.

The United States has run trade deficits since the early 1970s, meaning America has been privileged with consuming more than we produce for half a century![89] They build, we consume, that's my motto and it's been the unsaid motto of not only American, but global elitists for decades.

As long as wealth transfers from the poor and middle class to the political donor class, it doesn't matter if world hunger is solved or justice is served. What matters is that powerful men get what they want without being questioned.

I can't help but laugh when Americans burn down cities around the nation, protesting for minority rights when minorities are being taken advantage of around the world so entitled social justice warriors in America can live off the system. If people only knew how the world really operates, they would be directing their frustration at globalists.

A good president keeps the reality of global injustice hidden from the people; the Kennedy family found this out the hard way. From opposing the military industrial complex to tampering with monetary policy in an effort to make federal reserve notes backed by silver bullion through Executive Order 11110,[90] President Kennedy simply couldn't be trusted to execute the objectives of globalists.

November 22, 1963 was a pivotal day in our nation's history. When the honorable Lyndon Baines Johnson took over as President, powerful men could trust the Oval Office would protect their interests once again. Proven politicians who get things done for the well-being of the richest men in the world are needed in the White House and elitist-willing, someday that chosen person will be me.

In a globalist society, everyone is used or taken advantage of, including me. I know my role, I'm a pawn on the chess board for the most powerful people in the world and I do what is expected of me. As a strong, power-hungry woman, I've chosen a life of complacency at the highest level over apathy and inaction.

World Economic Forum

Advancements in transportation and technology since the turn of the 20th century have made conquering the world within the realm of possibility for the first time in history. The Ottoman and Roman Empires could only extend so far. While it used to take people years to travel across the greatest empires in the past, we can now feasibly travel to the other side of the globe in less than a day, especially with the use of private jets, like the ones I use.

Two world wars with mass casualties were needed before powerful men figured out how to stabilize a global society. Balancing foreign trade and wealth creation with foreign policy and the interests of weapons manufacturers is not an easy task. "Guns and butter" is a term economists use to state that a country has to balance their economic output between goods and services with weapons for war.

As a staunch advocate for gun-control, I understand the purpose of weapons is to control people and that law-abiding civilians need their rights suppressed in order to ensure we have the upperhand in ruling over them. Raytheon, Lockheed Martin, and other war profiteers need military conflict to expand their wealth.[91] Fortunately, BlackRock CEO and World Economic Forum (WEF) contributor Larry Fink sees the value in investing in instruments of war.[92]

Globalism takes a multi-faceted orchestration of manipulating the marketplace, sustaining military conflict, and controlling the thoughts and perspectives of differing cultures around the world. Politicians, businessmen, and philanthropists gather annually at the WEF to discuss how to manage a global economy. Only the most powerful and most complacent members of society get invited to this prestigious meeting of the minds.

They don't want politicians who think for themselves, but that doesn't mean they just want yes men either. The best politicians do what they are told and are able to sell the decisions globalists make to the public. Joe Biden is the best puppet elitists could hope for other than the fact that he isn't selling the globalist's agenda very well.

As someone who has what it takes to do what I am told and the capability to trick the people into believing I have their interest in mind, I'm a prime prospect for President of the United States. I accepted the invitation to partake in the WEF because the relationships I built while there have opened doors to gain the support I need to take over the keys to the United States government.

While participating in the WEF, a couple of my political heroes were also involved in the effort to guide and direct the global agenda. Al Gore, Vice President of the United States from 1993-2001 and Chairman and co-founder of Generation Investment Management, is one of the Board of Trustees for the WEF.[93] Brave men like Mr. Gore who are willing to put everything on the line to make sure powerful men get to control society deserve to be on the WEF board.

Former Democrat candidate for President, John Kerry, a regular WEF agenda contributor is involved in the discussion as well.[94] President Biden has assured Mr. Kerry a seat at the table in every imaginable globalist effort impacting the environment. Making sure reliable politicians rise through the ranks of decision making is a key objective. Mr. Kerry understands his assignment is to pretend to care about the environment but to make decisions the elitists want. Government created and taxpayer funded handouts for corporations that are environmentally friendly helps line the pockets of the rich while pandering to people who for whatever reason actually care about the environment.

Knowing I was surrounded by the world's most powerful movers and shakers made a chill go down my spine. Simply imagining myself as their top global pawn someday proves my self- interested decisions have brought me to the top stage of political conversations on the planet. The WEF will forever be able to put their trust in me to advance their agenda.[95]

Only the most worthy of politicians should be considered for President of the United States. My newly found global connections and willingness to conform to the status quo has put me in the driver's seat to be in charge of the United States.

Preventing people who haven't gotten the nod from the WEF from holding office is a core objective of our network. Keeping Donald Trump away from the Oval Office is priority number one, and I'm more than prepared to do everything within my power to see to it that Mr. Trump is left as far away from making global decisions as possible.

Dealing with The Donald

I would be remiss if I did not thank the political establishment for their unending support of my regime. The establishment helped me reach this office, and I thank them through loyalty to their agenda. I could not wage my campaign against liberty had it not been for the mainstream media. My friends in the press make it easy for me to do my job. They agree with me in my central planning mission, so they depict me as a true expert. No one is allowed to question my rhetoric and the media allows us to control the narrative.

With the narrative in our hands, we make every election, policy, and even every tweet a moral dilemma. Donald Trump is always depicted as the moral evil. We are the moral good because we said so. If Mr. Trump is as bad as we say he is, and we have made him out to be a monster, then any action or policy of ours is justified as a means of defeating The Orange Man. It's all a matter of perspective, that's why we fight so hard to control what is shared with the masses.

The media's constant harassment of Mr. Trump helps politicians such as myself increase our profile in the national media. When Tudor Dixon ran against me in the 2022 gubernatorial race, the media used her association with the former president against her. The media was easily able to lie, projecting their false criticisms of Mr. Trump onto Mrs. Dixon. It wasn't Gretchen vs. Tudor, it was Gretchen vs. MAGA extremism. Neither the media nor myself will ever admit that MAGA extremism is a lie. President Trump and his allies are devoted to restoring America to its domestic and international greatness.

My party opposes this mission. America is a mere opportunity for special interests to maximize their profits while power-hungry politicians such as myself exploit the system to consolidate power and bring tyranny to our country. I am the co- chairwoman for Joe Biden's re-election campaign.[96] I prioritize my party over the people. This is something that The Donald does not tolerate, which makes him dangerous to our agenda.

President Trump is too worried about bringing greatness to America. Our Democratic Party is busy bribing people to vote for our candidates instead of focusing on making the world a better place; we care nothing for greatness. We care nothing for unity. We only want power, and we will do anything necessary to gain or keep power.

Corruption is completely justifiable when we do it. The Biden family is corrupt to its core, but that won't stop me from working hard to force four more years of Biden on the American people. Corruption is necessary because if we weren't in charge, then Donald Trump would be President, and it would be a disaster for those of us looking to abuse the system for our own gain.

Donald Trump does not weaponize the mainstream media to deceive people into accepting his policies. He fights the lies in the media to bring truth to the American public. Truth brings down our entire house of cards. If the people knew we used fear to manipulate them, notably during the scamdemic, the FBI kidnapping hoax, and January 6th, then they would end our reign by voting against us.

We thrive off of fear. Mr. Trump and his associates value the truth over fear. He does not trust the science as we do. He believes in government accountability, which is a burden we would never place on any official. The Donald believes that the traditional American way of patriotic self-governance is good. He promises to drain the swamp, but the swamp runs much deeper than Washington DC. I am a swamp- dweller, a manipulative and controlling establishment politician, who seeks nothing more from public office than personal glory and enrichment.

The honorable President Joe Biden has been in government longer than the Ukraine of today has existed. President Biden's half century in public office is only proof of the expertise that is necessary to manage a population through government. He has played a role in Ukraine for decades now, helping to bring peace and stability to the region. As part of the Senate Foreign Relations Committee, then Senator Biden sponsored six pieces of legislation and co- sponsored 33 others in support of Ukraine, including attempting to create pathways for Ukraine to join NATO and the global empire of nations.

President Biden has always been a big fan of NATO while President Trump questioned NATO, something my bosses cannot allow. Before The Donald took office, Joe Biden spent his time as Vice President being the "point person on Ukraine" during the Barack Hussein Obama administration. He even visited the country six times. I have a lot to learn from Joe when it comes to deception. He and his team brag about his sponsorship of "anti-corruption" initiatives in Ukraine, claiming he worked with high-ranking government officials to create a cleaner political environment.[97]

This was a total lie, but many believed it. In a phone call with Petro Poroshenko, Ukraine's President at the time, Mr. Biden told him "anything you can do to push the Privatbank to closure so that the IMF loan comes forward, I would respectfully suggest is critically important to your economic as well as physical security."[98] Once again, masterful use of manipulation by my boss. Mr. Biden floated the possibility of Poroshenko being assassinated if he did not comply with his request, which would ensure globalist grip on Ukraine's finances. He also bragged about getting a top corruption prosecutor fired for actually doing his job. What the prosecutor didn't understand was that we do not occupy high level positions to actually do good for our people. We are too smart for that. Our mission is to get rich at all costs as the Biden family has done.

Using our friends in the mainstream media, nearly every Democrat swore that Hunter Biden's laptop was not real. Sure, compromising documents of Hunter Biden engaging in many illicit activities were found on the laptop, but that's a matter of private life. Hunter Biden is the victim who was inexplicably dragged through a court process that was a political witch-hunt. You should feel sorry for him. It's not easy to make six figures a month stirring up chaos in Ukraine and building a lucrative relationship with the mayor of Moscow's wife.[99] Simply doing nothing productive, causing global chaos, and smoking his life away through a crack pipe is nothing short of admirable. We fought hard for the boss's son, and continue to do so even when the law cannot ignore his crimes.[100]

Sometimes the mainstream media isn't enough to convince the people of a lie. They need the experts. Luckily, 50 intelligence agents reviewed Hunter Biden's laptop and declared that it, "has all the classic earmarks of a Russian information operation."[101] This is a common theme in the Democratic Party. We spent years accusing Mr. Trump of Russian collusion. He was absolved of all charges because we were lying, which could have been a major blow to our party if it weren't for media assistance. As Mr. Trump was believed to be a Russian asset, he was wrongfully discredited in the process, and Democratic involvement in Eastern Europe was able to continue to set the foundation for immense turmoil. Unfortunately, the courts failed us. The serial number of the laptop matched the serial number Apple provided in its subpoena, which factually confirmed that Hunter Biden and his family were the problem all along.[102]

Hunter Biden's laptop has been a five year firestorm in the media. Democrats and deep state operatives have worked tirelessly to discredit any attempts to bring the contents of the laptop to light. We claimed it was Russian disinformation. When that failed, we pivoted to the privacy standpoint. We in the Democratic Party do care about privacy when it pertains to the criminal son of our President. We also tried to make Hunter appear to be a sympathetic individual, as difficult as that must sound. However, the documents became public when Hunter Biden's laptop was leaked. Hunter described his relationship to Burisma, a Ukrainian oil and gas corporation by saying, "The Biden name is synonymous with democracy and transparency, and that's why I said it was gold to [Burisma]."[103] Hunter admitted to using his last name for profit. He was the son of the Vice President, so he could leverage his way into any high-paying position. The Bidens represent democracy, meaning some of the highest offices in the land can be sold off to foreign lobbies and special interests.

The Foreign Agents Registration Act (FARA), was designed to promote transparency, the same quality Hunter attributed to his last name. Hunter's presence in Ukraine was corrupt, but Democrats were able to manipulate legal loopholes[104] to justify his salary. FARA was exploitable, and that is exactly what Hunter did, giving him the concealment of plausible deniability. The establishment loves double standards. Hunter Biden's laptop is to be safeguarded while President Trump is to be the constant source of scrutiny.

The Biden family has a history of being abusive and perverted towards women and children. Hunter Biden's laptop contains many encounters with prostitutes, as well as his relationship with his deceased brother's wife.[105] Though this is not ideal, the apple didn't fall far from the tree. There are many photos of children seeming uncomfortable around Joe Biden.[106] That is not a concern though, the kids just do not know yet to unconditionally trust their leaders.

This is clearly the fault of parents for not telling their children to trust the government. The venerable President Biden has always been a hands-on type of politician, seeking to anoint people with his presence. This is a common trait within the highest ranking

Democrats. Joe takes it to a whole new level. Ashley Biden's diary has an entry that discusses trauma, including, "Showers with my dad (probably not appropriate)."[107]

Why was Joe Biden showering with his daughter? She clearly feels discomfort thinking about it. The Democrats do not care about Ashley Biden's trauma. Similarly, we do not care about Hunter's crack addiction. What we care about is keeping their dad in power, because that helps people like me advance my career.

Joe Biden is the lead anti-Trump Democrat, but he is chock full of corruption and scandals. Although he has baggage, we need him. Who else could get away with being complicit in so much corruption other than a confused elderly man who should be in a nursing home? We turn a blind eye to the actions of his storied life.

While the Republicans wrestle with whether or not they claim Donald Trump, we on the left laugh at their disunity. Really, it should be a non-brainer. If the Republicans want to truly challenge us, they should rally behind President Trump. It seems that some of them do not want to challenge us. To that I say the more the merrier. I love political opponents with no real unity or organization. They are easy for me to manage because they offer no real resistance to my rule.

I love obedience, whether it comes from enthusiasm for me or over a shared hatred of The Orange Man. The Democrats move as one well- oiled, well-funded machine. We have factions within our party, but we do our best to not bring these conflicts to the public eye. We need the public to understand that they need to vote blue no matter who, which in effect means the American people can count on any one of us to promote the same miserable policies.

There are progressives, and then there are even further radical progressives. But we all have something in common; we love big government, and we remember that we sit on the same side of the aisle. We do not use the media to attack our own like the Republicans. That would be the dumbest thing we could do, thankfully we have establishment Republicans for that. Our party system works in lockstep. When I became governor, the Democrats flocked to me. I enjoyed receiving the endorsement of Joe Biden, which actually came as a benefit to me. I also frequently fail to represent factions of Democrats in my own state, yet they know when I involve myself in corporate elitism, they are to fall in line and support me.

Mitt Romney, the Republican candidate in the presidential election preceding President Trump, was a moderate and corporate elitist who lost. In other words, he was our favorite brand of Republican. Mr. Romney does not challenge us in any significant way. Republicans like him are willing to vote for us to maintain some image of pragmatic bipartisanship. We would never do the same for them, but their folly is our gain. We will occasionally shout at one another, but at the end of the day Republicans like Mr. Romney have more in common with us than they do the American people. For example, Mitt Romney supported Joe Biden in the 2020 Presidential Election, even though it was a private endorsement. His biographer, McKay Croppins, said, "But in private, he made little effort to conceal the fact that he was pulling for Joe Biden."[108] That's what we love to hear, Mr. Romney! Perhaps one of my own many lies was useful in bringing the corrupt senator to Democratic territory, but what really matters is our shared hatred of Donald Trump.

Mr. Romney was not alone. Many in the 2016 Republican primary hated President Trump, either admittedly or in private. John Kasich, one such hopeful for the 2016 bid, sided with us in his disdain for President Trump. We prefer Mr. Kasich to Mr. Romney because Mr. Kasich actively undermined the president and leader of his own party. He made life easier for all of us here on the Democratic campaign trail. The best part was that Mr. Kasich did not even want anything in return.

He's essentially a Democrat in disguise. He voiced his thoughts on President Trump saying, "When I took on Trump, from the beginning, refused to endorse him, refused to go to the convention, endorsed Joe Biden, I'm not calling myself out as a great leader. But what I'll say is: So what? I did what I felt I had to do."[109] I am starting to think Joe Biden is more popular among establishment Republicans than any other demographic. Mr. Kasich is an example of an establishment politician hard-at-work, promoting the uniparty transformation of our country.

Chris Christie has been a staunch Democrat-in-disguise for at least eight years, easily identifiable by his persistent anti-Trump history. I don't think the 2016 primary ever ended for Christie, as he still takes every opportunity to bash Donald Trump. That's alright with me, the more establishment Republicans virtue signal by expressing their disdain for Donald Trump, the more fractured their party becomes.

We need every anti-Trump voice we can get. Our hysteria runs deep, and we need you, the people, to help fan the flames for tyranny. The establishment's unified anti-Trump talking points are supposed to isolate people like you from Mr. Trump. Politicians like Christie, Kasich, and Romney are all divisive, which makes them prime Democratic assets. Mr. Christie's commitment that, "The only thing I will commit to is: I'm not voting for Trump under any circumstances,"[110] is an example of the type of internal sabotage my party does not face.

Lawfare

Lawfare is a familiar Democratic strategy, one that is the byproduct of bureaucratic governance. The process is the punishment, as usually these lawsuits drag on for years. Even if the outcome is favorable to our enemy, they will likely be financially ruined and spiritually drained by the process. Donald Trump is different. He has more resources than the average business owner. We hate Mr. Trump because he represents the classic sense of American values. He often proclaims his belief in America First. Small business owners try to live the reality of America First, as they attempt to exercise their freedom by selling a product or service to their neighbors for a fair price. My policies, as well as those of my colleagues, have brought forward the globalist agenda of open borders, emergency rule, environmental tyranny, abortion, and rule by experts rather than self-governance.

In 2020, Democrats led the sham trial to impeach President Trump over an alleged quid pro quo with Ukraine. They got their wish, and we sought to tarnish his legacy through the impeachment process. Of course, our candidate to run against Mr. Trump was actually guilty of corruption in Eastern Europe. As Vice President, Joe Biden just so happened to be politically involved in Ukraine, where his son, Hunter, received exorbitant compensation for sitting on the board of Burisma. If anyone was doing backdoor deals with Ukraine, it would have been one of the Bidens. President Biden has since launched a proxy war to send hundreds of billions of US dollars to Ukraine with no strategic gain and nothing to show but the immeasurable cost of Ukrainian lives lost. President Biden repeatedly sends more and more US resources to Ukraine, even when there is no reason except to fund the military industrial complex.

Perpetual war is needed to keep our opponents at bay. Whether they be foreign or domestic, applying constant pressure is of utmost importance. That's why we haven't stopped trying to discredit, impeach, and handcuff President Trump for nine years, culminating in the kangaroo court in New York.

Mr. Trump was convicted on all 34 counts and is now a convicted felon. This means we have won. We weaponized the legal system against a former President. Waging lawfare against Mr. Trump is the new Democratic strategy for the 2024 presidential election. Who needs a man- made virus outbreak or Marxist Black Lives Matter movement when you can rig up charges against your opponent and get the desired outcome?

This is a critical election for my party, as I explained, "Right now, we know, in this country, there is a stark choice in front of us between a president who respects the rule of law and a former president who is a convicted felon who wants to use the implements of government to go after his enemies and is running on vengeance and grievance as his platform."""" Yes, that's it, Donald Trump is the candidate of vengeance. It's my party and the media that goes after him for nearly a decade, but Mr. Trump is the one who is vengeful. Get it?

What this really means is that we are terrified of a second term for President Trump. He wants to put an end to our reign of deception. This cannot happen. America cannot be great again. The globalists line our pockets, not hardworking patriots. We persecute Mr. Trump and then tell you that he is the one you need to fear. That's because we are the real criminals. We are the liars. We lied about Mr. Trump from the start. We lied about the man-made virus. We even lied about January 6th as there were many federal agents on the scene instigating the situation. We have lied to you about everything ranging from Mr. Trump's legitimacy as President to my personal travel vacations during the illegal shutdowns. But, surely our lies are far better than reading "mean tweets" from a president. Under our control, there will be no mean tweets from anyone. Love is love and you will remember that.

Mean tweets are unacceptably hateful. How could anyone be so distasteful? Social media is a tool to spread lies and crackdown on free-thinkers. It is not the place to speak independently and honestly about political issues. Since The Donald does this and we do not, he is divisive. Mean tweets are violent because words hurt too. I would know, as I am far more concerned about what the President posts on twitter than the safety of Michigan's cities during the peaceful protests of 2020.

My party is quick to accuse Donald Trump of violent rhetoric. This is a classic case of projection, as the Democratic Party is the true party of division and violence. Accusing Donald Trump serves as the perfect coverup for our own nefarious interests. Creative play, almost as if we read *Rules for Radicals* by Saul Alinsky!

When writing about the kidnapping hoax, I described the former president by saying, "Trump just keeps going, hostile as ever. He is trying to distract Americans from his failure to protect our families and trying to divide us further to win the election. He has taken to Twitter to spread lies and launch cheap insults against those with whom he disagrees."[112] Donald Trump is the violent one, by his very existence he instigated the plot against me and he knows it.

Violent Protests

The Democrats supported "peaceful protests" in 2020. I have no issue with political riots so long as it advances my party's interests. Cities nationwide were burned and looted in the name of equity. We can justify any action with the equity label. That's the strategy of my party.

The president was the real source of chaos, not our inability to maintain order. We charged President Trump as an insurrectionist and depicted him as a demagogue attempting to overthrow our institutions when we were the ones who sought the overthrow of representative government. President Trump was too popular among the people. We chose to tear him down at every point because we do not believe in the people or their ability to govern. We know that government gives us the opportunity to expand our own powers as well as to enrich our special interest friends.

January 6, 2021 marked full-force manipulation against Donald Trump. We took a legitimate complaint, the security of the 2020 presidential election, and made it into a fringe topic. With federal agents and collaborators spread all about, many descended upon the Capitol. Among those was Ray Epps, who told people around him that, "we need to go into the Capitol."[113] Mr. Epps incited violence, encouraging people to break into the Capitol, which produced bad optics that Democrats were then able to use to turn people against "MAGA extremists." Mr. Epps sent a text claiming "I orchestrated it"[114] in reference to January 6. His urging of everyone to go inside certainly confirms it. People like Mr. Epps are very useful. They are rogue actors who help us control the narrative. Yet to this very day we hang the events of January 6th over President Trump's head. We censor information such as Mr. Epps' involvement and Nancy Pelosi's failure to secure extra law enforcement at the Capitol to make it more believable that we are the victims of President Trump's supposedly violent, divisive rhetoric."[115]

Also on the scene was John Sullivan, the founder of Insurgence USA. He was awfully excited to break into the window of the Capitol, egging on others even after Ashli Babbitt was shot and killed. Sullivan told bystanders that "it's time for a revolution!"[116] He claimed to be a journalist covering the event. I will say he is the best journalist we could ask for. Instead of reporting on events as they happened, Mr. Sullivan planted himself in the middle of the action and encouraged others towards disruption. He incited violence, which bolstered our false narrative.

As it turns out, Mr. Sullivan was also a supporter of progressive ideology. He explained that he "definitely believe[s] Black Lives Matter."[117] What do the events of January 6th have in common with a supporter of the Marxist Black Lives Matter movement? In both cases, Democrats encourage violence. Mr. Sullivan, the leftist ideologue, and Mr. Epps, who is believed to be a federal intelligence asset, are just two examples of unique individuals calling for increased force on January 6th. We appreciate their contributions, as we immediately tied these rogue actors to President Trump.

When American cities burned in the summer of 2020 in the name of racial equity, we did not condemn these actions. Instead, we applauded their bravery because we felt their antics supplemented our tactics. The media even lied to the public that the burning and looting of cities around our nation was the result of "mostly peaceful protests." Violence is a great aid to our agenda, and when we manipulate the people's actions, it gives the Democrats further control over the narrative, strengthening our lies to the American people.

Conquering the World

Democrats used to be the party of the people. Decades ago, large corporations simply wanted lower taxes for the rich and a business- friendly environment to help increase their profit margins.

The politics were relatively simple. Corporate America supported Republicans who wanted lower taxes for the rich. Believing that it was a net gain for everyone to have a business- friendly environment, Republican voters agreed with this vision. Democrats, on the other hand, had a stronghold on the unions and the worker rights movement, believing the people were being exploited by rich men who simply wanted to line their pockets with more and more money.

President John Fitzgerald Kennedy (JFK) was the last Democrat President to have a vision for America that resembled what the founding fathers had in store for our country. He challenged the military industrial complex, the corrupt banking system, and genuinely cared about the well-being of the people. We all know how that worked out for him. Lines of people in the streets eager to catch a glimpse of him meant nothing when he was incapable of finishing out his term because he was too extreme.

Fortunately, one of the greatest presidents of all time, Lyndon Baines Johnson (LBJ), was able to assume the position in the Oval

Office and control the direction of our country, ensuring prosperity for our wealthiest friends.

In 1965, the wage disparity between corporate elite CEOs and their employees was 20 to 1. A CEO deserves far more than 20 times as much compensation as a janitor. LBJ and his closest allies were able to launch a trend of ensuring CEOs get their fair share. By 2021, the wage disparity had grown to 399 to 1 for our best CEOs.[118]

Any logical person can tell you this rapid increase in wage disparity is not because of free markets. The more the government gives special handouts and tax breaks, while regulating small businesses out of the market, the more companies consolidate, accept defeat, and turn over their profits to those who are most obedient to the political machine. A compensation of 27.8 million dollars per year for a top CEO compared to 69,500 dollars for one of their employees is the product of central planning.

Those who wrongfully believe wage disparity in recent decades has been caused by free markets need to take a basic economics class. Anything is possible when the right narrative has enough funding, such as deceiving society into believing free markets are the cause of their problems.

The more complicated the system becomes, the more uncomfortable people are standing up for justice. When it takes an expert to formulate an advanced perspective on how government involvement is impacting the overall quality of life, the people are doomed to servitude.

If society wants to stop the rapid rise of tyranny and redistribution of wealth to the politically connected, they are going to have to realize status quo politicians including Mitt Romney, Hillary Clinton, Barack Hussein Obama, Joe Biden, and myself can't be trusted to change how public policy works.

Businesses, media, and powerful people who wittingly or unwittingly contribute to the erosion of liberty lose their spoils if politicians straighten out the government. When people simply look out for their own interests and the government is able to change the rules of the game, big government and the corporations that grow up around it win at the expense of everyone else.

Ultimately, politicians are responsible for creating and maintaining the status quo system of government taking from the people and giving to the donor class. Although there are only a select few of us who are the most corrupt, 95 percent of legislators and governors conform to the status quo and the remaining five percent are ostracized. The ruling elite don't support Bernie Sanders, not just because he's not a deep state operative, but because his ideas are terrible. Fortunately for him, Democrat politicians do our best to never publicly attack fellow Democrats, especially those to our left on the political spectrum. Instead we use radical left extremism to our advantage and with corporate media assistance, we have been quite successful.

Republican politicians are foolish and consistently try to prevent the best conservatives from winning in the Republican primary. Watching the Republican Party drift to the left as Democrats keep moving the goalposts further left year after year, decade after decade, has been a dream come true not just for me but for anyone who believes in central planning. JFK would be more conservative than most Republican politicians these days who have fallen into the trap of complacency with the corrupt establishment. A free market with less rules, regulations, taxes, fines, and fees does not create an atmosphere conducive for taking advantage of other people. The more the government does to create conflicts of interest and reduce freedom, the better off globalists become.

People pondering how the world could have so many emotional and economic issues with all the advancements in society simply don't have a clue how the real world works. It's not because of a lack of intelligence that the government keeps messing up, it's because it's not our objective.

Getting rich and donating to politicians is the best way to begin making a difference in the world. The best lobbyists invest millions of dollars into getting billions of dollars in corporate subsidies for themselves. It's truly one of the best investment schemes out there. Diverting corporate focus in a broken system toward taking advantage of other people assists in the ultimate objective of taking over the world.

Whether it's indoctrinating the youth or destroying the farming industry, the government stands by ready, willing, and able to take advantage of the people. Christianity and the nuclear family continue to pose a threat to our agenda and complicate our efforts. Infiltrating the church and perverting the message of the Bible has been a useful tool in disrupting the influence Christianity used to have in guiding a person's way of life. The more people feel jaded by sound Christian doctrine, and accepted by the government and false doctrine, the more they will put their trust in us to guide and direct their paths.

Lost and confused people continue to try to find truth in all the wrong places as the family unit continues to deteriorate. Stealth government operations have doomed millions of people to a life of depression and other mental health issues.

As society continues down the path of confusion and folly, they become easier to control. We cause the problems, people suffer, people turn to the government for solutions, and we make decisions for them, yet somehow they feel free.

Like a shackled prisoner with limited chances remaining to escape, our country and the rest of the world are going to have to put their trust in a Savior who has capabilities greater than man. With the trajectory society is on, elitists will soon rule over the world in a way we have never seen before.

With the foundation for global domination set by shadowy figures most of the world wouldn't even recognize, I will remain a puppet for those far more powerful than me. Yet if we get our way, I will be the one credited with accomplishing the unthinkable. By the time my political career is finished, I will have left such an impact on a global scale, there won't be a person alive who won't know the True Gretchen and the story about my rise to power.

Letter to Gretchen

July 4, 2024

Gretchen,

Twelve years ago I was a young and ambitious man, ready and eager to make a difference in the world. Coming up with solutions for the problems facing society quickly became my hobby.

Having listened to my thoughts and ideas for years as if it was a second job, my dad pushed me to apply myself in a way other than driving him insane by constantly talking to him about whatever was on my mind. With nothing better to do, trying to figure out how to end world hunger and fighting for liberty and justice was my top priority. Not just my dad, but those closest to me, volunteered their time listening to my ideas.

Just out of college and ready to tackle the biggest problems facing society, I was fully skeptical of elected officials, lobbyists, and status quo politics, believing almost everyone involved was corrupt. My opinion of corruption in government was that the people in it were evil, malicious, had bad intentions, and simply didn't care about anyone else.

Having been inspired by my hero Ron Paul, I felt called to run for office myself so I could break apart the machine from within to restore freedom for the people. Although my position on the issues has not changed, my perception of people in government has changed.

Being a staff member for three years and now a legislator for nearly four years has helped me to see the entire process differently. I trust the intentions of my colleagues far more than I would have imagined. The problem is that the system is corrupt and well-intentioned people lose their way without even noticing what happened.

Complications with politics as usual have existed throughout history. You are not the source of the problem. Quite frankly, you have navigated the world of politics very well and could end up becoming President of the United States someday. However, your actions are the product of a corrupt system that incentivizes complacent operations, and it is those actions with which I and many others take issue.

Regardless of what is in store for your future, I encourage you to reflect on the underlying truths of this book. It is clear that you and I have ideological differences, but I hope you can see that we have more than just simple disagreements on policy and the proper role of government. While the book is satirical in nature, its message is not a joke. It is intended to help restore and preserve essential freedom.

I understand this book will offend you, but I hope and pray it convicts you to reflect on the damage done to society by status quo politics and that you will rise above the temptation to continue conforming with the political system. Corruption in politics is pervasive, but not insurmountable.

I'll read your book if you read mine and maybe someday we can discuss the proper role of government and future plans to protect the God- given rights of the people. Your Grandma Nino taught you to see the good in everyone[119] and although my book is critical and thought- provoking, I hope you can see the good in me and my intentions in this parody.

In Liberty,

Steve Carra

Steve Carra

State Representative District 36

Chair of the Michigan House Freedom Caucus

Endnotes

My Rise to Power

[1] Weber, E. B. (n.d.). Gretchen Whitmer, Grand Rapids, MI Michigan currently in East Lansing, MI. Gretchen Whitmer. https://www.classcreator.com/Grand-Rapids-MI-Forest-Hills-Central-1989/class_profile.cfm?member_id=1760792

The Man-Made Virus Outbreak

[2] Wolf, N. (2023, March 6). What's in the Pfizer Documents? [Video]. Hillsdale College. https://freedomlibrary.hillsdale.edu/programs/cca-iv-big-pharma/what-s-in-the-pfizer-documents

[3] Schachtel, J. (2023, March 6). Big Pharma and Big Government [Video]. Hillsdale College. https://freedomlibrary.hillsdale.edu/programs/cca-iv-big-pharma/big-pharma-and-big-government

[4] Lama, D. (2020, July 18). FOX 35 INVESTIGATES: Questions raised after fatal motorcycle crash listed as COVID-19 death. FOX 35 Orlando. https://www.fox35orlando.com/news/fox-35-investigates-questions-raised-after-fatal-motorcycle-crash-listed-as-covid-19-death

[5] Mann, E. A., Rompicherla, S. Gallagher, M. P. Alonso, G. T. Fogel, N. R. Simmons, J. Wood, J. R. Wong, J. C. Noor, N. Gomez, P. Daniels, M. & Ebekozien, O. (2022). Comorbidities increase COVID 19 hospitalization in young people with type 1 diabetes. Pediatric Diabetes, 23(7), 968–975. https://doi.org/10.1111/pedi.13402

[6] Ibid.

[7] Hermes, G. (2021, May 25). Michigan nursing homes rewarded thousands of dollars after not following COVID protocols. WDIV. https://www.clickondetroit.com/news/local/2021/05/

[8] Erb, R. (2020, September 16). In tense hearing, Whitmer official defends MI COVID nursing home strategy. Bridge Michigan. https://www.bridgemi.com/michigan-health-watch/tense-hearing-whitmer-official-defends-mi-covid-nursing-home-strategy

[9] Hermes, G. Michigan nursing homes rewarded thousands of dollars after not following COVID protocols.

[10] Ibid.

[11] Jackson, C. (2022, December 6). Pfizer to invest $750 million in Kalamazoo area operation. WEMU-FM. https://www.wemu.org/michigan-news/2022-12-06/pfizer-to-invest-750-million-in-kalamazoo-area-operation12

[12] Whitmer still claiming vaccine credit from subsidy for unbuilt Pfizer facility. (n.d.). Michigan Capitol Confidential. https://www.michigancapitolconfidential.com/whitmer-still-claiming-vaccine-credit-from-subsidy-for-unbuilt-pfizer-facility

[13] Office of the Commissioner. (2024, May 21). Emergency use authorization. U.S. Food And Drug Administration. https://www.fda.gov/emergency-preparedness-and-response/mcm-legal-regulatory-and-policy-framework/emergency-use-authorization

[14] 10 Rules for Responding to Pandemics: Learning from Michigan's COVID-19 Experience Learning from Michigan's COVID-19 Experience on JSTOR. (n.d.). www.jstor.org.

https://www.jstor.org/stable/resrep49359?sid=primo&saml_data=eyJzYW1sVG9rZW4iOilwZjIyMTc2Nio3NmRhLTQzNzYtYTYwZS04NjVkZDUxMjY0OTUiLCJpbnNoaXR1dGlvbklkcyl6WyJlMjUyMDk5My1Yzky LTQ1YTYtYTMyNC0wYWM1Y2UoMjBjYWQiXXo&seq=1

[15] Ibid

[16] John Agar. (2021, March 19). Jailed Michigan restaurant owner 'drawing the line' against unfair state orders, backers say. Mlive. https://www.mlive.com/news/grand-rapids/2021/03/jailed-michigan-restaurant-owner-drawing-the-line-against-unfair-state-orders-backers-say.html?outputType=amp

[17] Michigan restaurant owner in jail for defying virus orders | AP News. (2021, March 19). AP News. https://apnews.com/article/arrests-michigan-coronavirus-pandemic-holland-208f8d19c60910e1943d725ba804e47e

[18] The Center Square. (2021, April 8). COVID-19 small business closures in Michigan pegged at 39.7%. The Center Square. https://www.thecentersquare.com/michigan/article_ef57068c-972e-11eb-a726-6755f20fb618.html

[19] Detroit Regional Chamber. (2022, April 29). U.S. Census survey shows Michigan's small businesses hardest hit by COVID-19. Detroit Regional Chamber. https://www.detroitchamber.com/u-s-census-survey-shows-michigans-small-businesses-hardest-hit-by-covid-19/

[20] Dunleavy, K. (2024, February 22). While Moderna moves off COVID, Spikevax posts market-share gains on Pfizer rival. Fierce Pharma. https://www.fiercepharma.com/pharma/while-moderna-moving-covid-its-vaccine-gaining-share-pfizers-comirnaty#:~:text=During%20their%20heyday%20in%202021,versus%20%2436%20billion%20for%20Spikevax.

[21] Ibid.

[22] Martínez-Beltrán, S. (2021, April 20). Michigan Gov. Whitmer defends her Florida trip, calls criticism 'maddening' Bridge MI. https://www.bridgemi.com/michigan-government/michigan-gov-whitmer-defends-her-florida-trip-calls-criticism-maddening?amp.

Rules for Thee, Not for Me

[23] Martínez-Beltrán, S. (2021, April 20). Michigan Gov. Whitmer defends her Florida trip, calls criticism 'maddening' Bridge MI. https://www.bridgemi.com/michigan-government/michigan-gov-whitmer-defends-her-florida-trip-calls-criticism-maddening?amp

[24] Neumann, S. (2021, May 24). Mich. Gov. Gretchen Whitmer Apologizes After Photo Shows Her In Violation Of State's COVID Rule. Peoplemag. https://people.com/politics/gretchen-whitmer-apologizes-after-photo-shows-her-in-violation-of-states-covid-rule/

[25] Noor, P. (2020, July 1). Michigan governor's husband under fire for asking to take his boat out during lockdown. Michigan | the Guardian.

https://amp.theguardian.com/us-news/2020/may/26/gretchen-whitmer-husband-marc-mallory-boat-lockdown

The Kidnapping Hoax

[26] Ciaramella, C. (2022, September 1). Whitmer kidnapping plot just one example of FBI entrapment. Reason.com. https://reason.com/2022/09/04/its-almost-always-the-feds/

[27] Burnett, S., Tarm, M., & White, E. (2022, March 9). Lawyers: FBI lured men for Michigan Gov. Whitmer kidnap plot | AP News. AP News. https://apnews.com/article/whitmer-kidnap-plot-trial-a7dd7bc1a4e5917c3e2c78f599ebc17f

[28] Sullum, J. (2022, April 13). FBI's tactics doomed case against men charged in kidnapping plot of Michigan governor - Chicago Sun-Times. Chicago Sun-Times. https://chicago.suntimes.com/columnists/2022/4/13/23023950/michigan-governor-gretchen-whitmer-kidnapping-plot-acquittal-fbi-entrapment-jacob-sullum-column

[29] Burnett, S., Tarm, M., & White, E. Lawyers: FBI lured men for Whitmer kidnap plot

[30] Sullum, J. FBI's tactics doomed case against men charged in kidnapping ploy

[31] Ibid.

[32] Aabram, V., & Aabram, V. (2021, December 22). Ex-FBI agent who led Whitmer kidnapping plot investigation pleads no contest in assault of wife - Washington Examiner. Washington Examiner - Political News and Conservative Analysis About Congress, the President, and the Federal Government. https://www.washingtonexaminer.com/news/773782/ex-fbi-agent-who-led-whitmer-kidnapping-plot-investigation-pleads-no-contest-in-assault-of-wife/?utm_source=google&utm_medium=cpc&utm_campaign=WE_Pmax_Section-Policy&gad_source=1&gclid=CjoKCQjw3tCyBhDBARIsAEYoXNnUyjgcW7e1oHRbSEqBOVeY9OeGN4ZQWTYCZeoN4XBArX-UKYCTS_gaAlEOEALw_wcB#google_vignette

[33] Beaman, J., & Beaman, J. (2023, November 3). Key FBI agent in Whitmer kidnapping plot posted anti-Trump rants online during investigation - Washington Examiner. Washington Examiner - Political News and Conservative Analysis About Congress, the President, and the Federal Government. https://www.washingtonexaminer.com/news/540622/key-fbi-agent-in-whitmer-

kidnapping-plot-posted-anti-trump-rants-online-during-investigation/

[34] Ciaramella, C. Whitmer kidnapping plot just one example of FBI entrapment

[35] Burnett, S., Tarm, M., & White, E. Lawyers: FBI lured men for Whitmer kidnap plot

[36] Whitmer, G. (2020, October 27). The plot to kidnap me. The Atlantic. https://www.theatlantic.com/ideas/archive/2020/10/plot-kidnap-me/616866/

[37] Ibid.

[38] Nessel, FBI silent in face of obvious voter fraud discovered by clerks. (2024, February 14). Mi House Repubs. https://gophouse.org/posts/nessel-fbi-silent-in-reply-to-obvious-voter-fraud-discovered-by-clerks

[39] Whitmer, G. The plot to kidnap me.

Indoctrination Camps

[40] Superintendent says Detroit schools "deeply using critical race theory." (n.d.). https://www.foxnews.com/us/superintendent-says-detroit-schools-deeply-using-critical-race-theory.print

[41] Parents Defending Education. (2023, February 7). Teachers at Gull Lake Community Schools promote communism and LGBTQ issues on social media - Parents Defending Education. https://defendinged.org/incidents/teachers-at-gull-lake-community-schools-promote-communism-and-lgbtq-issues-on-social-media/

[42] Ibid.

[43] Video exposes Kinsey Research Fund | EWTN. (n.d.). EWTN Global Catholic Television Network. https://www.ewtn.com/catholicism/library/video-exposes-kinsey-research-fund-4036

[44] Fraudulent Kinsey Sex Research. (n.d.). Familywatch.org. https://familywatch.org/fwi/Kinsey_fraud.cfm

[45] Video exposes Kinsey Research Fund

[46] Anderson, C. (2021, August 2). "Diversity" group linked to Swing-District DEM pushes for critical race theory in Michigan schools. Washington Free Beacon. https://freebeacon.com/elections/diversity-group-linked-to-swing-district-dem-

pushes-for-critical-race-theory-in-michigan-schools/

[47] Zimmerman, K. (2023, August 14). Michigan schools take different approaches to LGBTQ policies. WCMU Public Radio. https://radio.wcmu.org/local-regional-news/2023-08-14/michigan-schools-take-different-approaches-to-lgbtq-policies

[48] Ibid.

[49] Parents Defending Education. Teachers at Gull Lake Community Schools promote LGBTQ issues

[50] Program on Intergroup Relations and the Spectrum Center, University of Michigan. (2021). Social Identity Wheel. In Adapted for Use by the Program on Intergroup Relations and the Spectrum Center, University of Michigan [Worksheet]. https://sites.lsa.umich.edu/inclusive-teaching/wp-content/uploads/sites/853/2021/12/Social-Identity-Wheel.pdf

[51] Runestad, J. (2023, February 23). Understanding the Elliot-Larsen Civil Rights Act and Senate Bill 4. Senatorjimrunestad.com. https://www.senatorjimrunestad.com/understanding-the-elliot-larsen-civil-rights-act-and-senate-bill-4/

Reproductive Tyranny

[52] The scientific consensus on when a human's life begins. (n.d.). PubMed. https://pubmed.ncbi.nlm.nih.gov/

[53] House Fiscal Agency. (2022). Ballot Proposal 3 of 2022 [Report]. https://www.house.mi.gov/hfa/PDF/Alpha/Ballot_Proposal_3_of_2022.pdf

[54] Skallman. (2022, September 29). FACT SHEET - The perils of Proposal 3 - Great Lakes Justice Center. Great Lakes Justice Center. https://www.greatlakesjc.org/fs_perils_of_prop_3/

[55] Jaslow, R. (2011, September 1). Abortion tied to sharp decline in women's mental health. CBS News. https://www.cbsnews.com/news/abortion-tied-to-sharp-decline-in-womens-mental-health/

[56] Oliver, A., & Oliver, A. (2024, June 1). Activists who blocked DC abortion clinic get combined 23 years in prison - Washington Examiner. Washington Examiner - Political News and Conservative Analysis About Congress, the President, and the Federal Government. https://www.washingtonexaminer.com/news/justice/3024975/activists-blocked-dc-

abortion-clinic-combined-23-years-prison/

[57] Ertelt, S. (2024, June 1). Joe Biden puts elderly woman in prison for 25 months for protesting abortion - LifeNews.com. LifeNews.com. https://www.lifenews.com/2024/05/31/joe-biden-puts-elderly-woman-in-prison-for-25-months-for-protesting-abortion/

[58] Di Fiore, B. (2024, June 4). Elderly pro-lifer's husband begs court for mercy as judge sentences ailing wife to prison. Live Action News. https://www.liveaction.org/news/elderly-prolifers-husband-begs-mercy-prison/

Environmental Injustice

[59] Rep. Fink: Green New Deal is a bad deal for Michigan. (2023, November 3). Mi House Repubs. https://gophouse.org/posts/rep-fink-green-new-deal-is-a-bad-deal-for-michigan

[60] Spartan Newsroom. (2023, December 8). High fertilizer costs hit Michigan farmers. https://news.jrn.msu.edu/2023/12/high-fertilizer-costs-hit-michigan-farmers/

[61] Ibid.

[62] Foreign Ownership of Michigan Farmland - Product Center. (n.d.). Product Center. https://www.canr.msu.edu/resources/foreign-ownership-of-michigan-farmland#:~:text=Foreign%20ownership%20in%20Michigan,-Most%20of%20the&text=Foreign%20ownership%20of%20Michigan%20agricultural,percent%20of%20all%20foreign%20ownership.

[63] Ellis, J. (2024, June 10). Who are the Largest Farmland Owners in the United States? Landgate. https://www.landgate.com/news/who-are-the-largest-farmland-owners-in-the-united-states#:~:text=Bill%20and%20Melinda%20Gates,Bill%20%26%20Melinda%20Gates%20Foundation%20Trust

[64] Galloway, M. (2021, December 10). Whose land is it anyway? Farmers, billionaires, foreign investors jockey for US farmland. Michigan Farm News. https://www.michiganfarmnews.com/whose-land-is-it-anyway-farmers-billionaires-foreign-investors-jockey-for-us-farmland

[65] Executive Order 2020-182: Council on Climate Solutions. (2020, September 23). https://www.michigan.gov/whitmer/news/state-orders-and-directives/2020/09/23/executive-order-2020-182

[66] Clark, L. E. & Michigan Department of Environment, Great Lakes, and Energy. (2022). [MI Healthy Climate Plan]. https://www.michigan.gov/egle/-/media/Project/Websites/egle/Documents/Offices/OCE/MI-Healthy-Climate-Plan.pdf?rev=d13f4adc2b1d45909bd708cafccbfffa&hash=99437BF2709B9B3471D16FC1EC692588

[67] Ibid.

[68] Kukulka, M. (2020, May 27). State sued dam owner for lowered lake levels before flooding. Midland Daily News. https://www.ourmidland.com/news/article/State-sued-dam-owner-for-lowered-lake-levels-15298695.php

[69] Garret Ellison. (2020, May 22). Failed dam owner fought with state over Wixom Lake levels before flood. Mlive. https://www.mlive.com/news/2020/05/owner-of-failed-dam-state-fought-over-wixom-lake-levels-before-flood.html?outputType=amp

[70] Kukulka, M. State sued dam owner for lowered lake levels

[71] Ibid.

[72] Michigan's renewable energy report card. (n.d.). Mackinac Center. https://www.mackinac.org/blog/2024/michigans-renewable-energy-report-card#:~:text=In%2520Michigan%252C%2520renewables%2520%E2%80%94%2520mostly%2520wind,%2520hydro%2520biomass%2520and%2520wind.

The Greatest Gift

[73] 14th Amendment. (n.d.). LII / Legal Information Institute. https://www.law.cornell.edu/constitution/amendmentxiv

[74] MCL - Article IV § 30 - Michigan Legislature. (n.d.). https://www.legislature.mi.gov/Laws/MCL?objectName=mcl-Article-IV-30

[75] Marbury v. Madison (1803). (2022, September 15). National Archives. https://www.archives.gov/milestone-documents/marbury-v-madison

[76] Scheck, T. (2020, December 8). How private money from Facebook's CEO saved the 2020 election. NPR. https://www.npr.org/2020/12/08/943242106/how-private-money-from-facebooks-ceo-saved-the-2020-election

[77] Rep. Steele: Budget surplus should mean lower taxes - Mi House Repubs. (2024, February 2). Mi House Repubs. https://gophouse.org/posts/rep-steele-budget-

surplus-should-mean-lower-taxes

[78] Oosting, J. (2023, March 28). Dana Nessel calls income tax cut temporary. Republicans express fury. Bridge Michigan. https://www.bridgemi.com/michigan-government/dana-nessel-calls-income-tax-cut-temporary-republicans-express-fury

[79] Business Subsidy Scorecard. (n.d.). Mackinac Center. https://www.mackinac.org/business-subsidies

[80] Gibbons, L. (2023, June 19). A liberal Democrat goes to Lansing. His principles are quickly put to the test. Bridge Michigan. https://www.bridgemi.com/michigan-government/liberal-democrat-goes-lansing-his-principles-are-quickly-put-test

[81] Witwer, Rep. & State of Michigan. (2023). Enrolled House Bill No. 4437. In Public Acts of 2023. https://www.legislature.mi.gov/documents/2023-2024/publicact/pdf/2023-PA-0119.pdf pg 255, 221

[82] Ibid.

[83] Ibid.

[84] China's biggest cobalt producer agrees to stop buying from individuals in DRC due to concerns over child labour - Business & Human Rights Resource Centre. (n.d.). Business & Human Rights Resource Centre. https://www.business-humanrights.org/en/latest-news/chinas-biggest-cobalt-producer-agrees-to-stop-buying-from-individuals-in-drc-due-to-concerns-over-child-labour/

[85] Rose White. (2023, October 16). Michigan gave millions to Ford's paused mega site project. What's been spent? Mlive. https://www.mlive.com/public-interest/2023/09/michigan-gave-millions-to-fords-paused-mega-site-project-whats-been-spent.html

[86] Enquirer, B. C. (2023, March 29). MAEDA receives $120.3M to support Ford's development of Marshall Megasite. Battle Creek Enquirer. https://www.battlecreekenquirer.com/story/news/2023/03/29/area-economic-development-alliance-receives-120-million-fords-development-of-marshall-megasite/70059595007/

[87] Lancaster, J. (2023, November 14). Michigan lawmakers signed NDAS, can't discuss corporate welfare scheme. Reason.com. https://reason.com/2023/11/14/michigan-lawmakers-signed-nondisclosure-agreements-cant-discuss-corporate-welfare-scheme/

Globalism

[88] Statista. (2024, April 15). U.S. Congress monthly public approval rating 2022-2024. https://www.statista.com/statistics/207579/public-approval-rating-of-the-us-congress/

[89] Reinbold, B., & Wen, Y. (2018, October 9). Understanding the Roots of the U.S. Trade Deficit. Federal Reserve Bank of St. Louis. https://www.stlouisfed.org/publications/regional-economist/third-quarter-2018/understanding-roots-trade-deficit

[90] Executive ORDER 11110—Amendment of Executive Order No. 10289 as amended, relating to the performance of certain functions affecting the Department of the Treasury | The American Presidency Project. (n.d.). https://www.presidency.ucsb.edu/documents/executive-order-11110-amendment-executive-order-no-10289-amended-relating-the-performance

[91] Fintel. (n.d.). BlackRock increases position in Raytheon Technologies (RTX). Nasdaq. https://www.nasdaq.com/articles/blackrock-increases-position-in-raytheon-technologies-rtx

[92] Laurence D. Fink - Agenda Contributor. (n.d.). World Economic Forum. https://www.weforum.org/agenda/authors/larry-fink/

[93] Leadership and governance. (n.d.). World Economic Forum. https://www.weforum.org/about/leadership-and-governance/

[94] John F. Kerry - Agenda Contributor. (n.d.). World Economic Forum. https://www.weforum.org/agenda/authors/john-kerry/

[95] What Whitmer said in Davos. (n.d.). Michigan Capitol Confidential. https://www.michigancapitolconfidential.com/analysis/what-whitmer-said-in-davos

Dealing with The Donald

[96] The Detroit News. (2024, June 9). Gov. Gretchen Whitmer says Trump is a convicted felon "running on vengeance." The Detroit News. https://www.detroitnews.com/story/news/politics/2024/06/09/gov-whitmer-says-trump-is-a-convicted-felon-running-on-vengeance/74035715007/

[97] Biden Has a Proven Track Record with Ukraine: What Can We Expect from His Administration? (n.d.). Wilson Center. https://www.wilsoncenter.org/blog-post/biden-has-proven-track-record-ukraine-what-can-we-expect-his-

administration

[98] Zubkova, D. (2020, May 20). Ex-U.S. Vice President Biden Asks Poroshenko To Accelerate Nationalization Of PrivatBank – Derkach Tapes. Ukrainian News. https://ukranews.com/en/news/703339-ex-u-s-vice-president-biden-asks-poroshenko-to-accelerate-nationalization-of-privatbank-derkach

[99] Devine, M., & Crane, E. (2022, October 17). Hunter Biden-linked real estate firm got at least $100M from Russian oligarch: sources. New York Post. https://nypost.com/2022/10/17/hunter-bidens-real-estate-firm-received-over-100m-from-russian-oligarch/

[100] Chase, R., Lauer, C., Kunzelman, M., Richer, A. D., & Long, C. (2024, June 11). Hunter Biden convicted of all 3 felonies in federal gun trial | AP News. AP News. https://apnews.com/article/hunter-biden-gun-trial-federal-charges-delaware-5dd8a9380235c6360a1ddb691ef24a06

[101] Mordock, J. (2024, June 4). FBI agent confirms authenticity of Hunter Biden's laptop. The Washington Times. https://www.washingtontimes.com/news/2024/jun/4/erika-jensen-confirms-authenticity-of-hunter-biden

[102] Ibid.

[103] Polo, M. (n.d.). Report on the Biden laptop. https://bidenreport.com/#p=141

[104] Polo, M. (n.d.-b). Report on the Biden laptop. https://bidenreport.com/#p=153

[105] John, A. (2024, June 10). Biden family's most intimate personal struggles put on display in court. CNN. https://www.cnn.com/2024/06/10/politics/biden-family-trial/index.html

[106] Richardson, V. (2023, November 19). 'Creepy Joe' charges resurface after Biden asks 6-year-old girl if she's 17. The Washington Times. https://www.washingtontimes.com/news/2023/nov/19/creepy-joe-biden-charges-resurface-after-he-asks-6/

[107] Tbs. (2024, May 13). Joe Biden accused of pedophilia with daughter Ashley's diary as alleged evidence. MARCA. https://amp.marca.com/en/lifestyle/us-news/presidential-election/2024/05/13/664244e9e2704e77688b457e.html

[108] Roche, L. R. (2024, May 16). Sen. Mitt Romney says his views are tiny 'chicken wing' of GOP. Deseret News. https://www.deseret.com/utah/2024/05/16/mitt-romney-msnbc-biden-trump-president-vote-pardon/

888888

[109] Fortinsky, S. (2023, July 18). Kasich urges GOP candidates to 'step up and say something' after Trump gets target letter. The Hill. https://thehill.com/homenews/campaign/4104088-kasich-urges-gop-candidates-to-step-up-and-say-something-after-trump-gets-target-letter/damp/?nxs-test=damp

[110] Robertson, N. (2024, February 8). Christie on Biden-Trump rematch: 'I'm not voting for Trump under any circumstances.' The Hill. https://thehill.com/homenews/campaign/4456275-christie-biden-trump-2024/mlite/?nxs-test=mlite

[111] The Detroit News. Whitmer says Trump is a convicted felon.

[112] Whitmer, G. The plot to kidnap me

[113] Impelli, M. (2024, January 10). Ray Epps' Jan. 6 sentence enrages MAGA. Newsweek. https://www.newsweek.com/ray-epps-january-6-sentence-enrages-maga-1859210

[114] Ibid.

[115] Oversight Subcommittee, (2024, June 10). Nancy Pelosi Blames Donald Trump for January 6th. [Video]. X. https://x.com/OversightAdmn/status/1800207258514575730/mediaViewer?currentTweet=1800207258514575730&currentTweetUser=OversightAdmn

[116] Palmer, E. (2022, February 20). Who is John Sullivan? Left-wing Activist Charged in Capitol Riot. Newsweek. https://www.newsweek.com/john-sullivan-capitol-attack-leftwing-antifa-1561898

[117] Ibid.

Conquering the World

[118] CEO pay has skyrocketed 1,460% since 1978: CEOs were paid 399 times as much as a typical worker in 2021. (n.d.). Economic Policy Institute. https://www.epi.org/publication/ceo-pay-in-2021/

Letter to Gretchen

[119] True Gretch. (n.d.). Book by Gretchen Whitmer | Official Publisher Page | Simon & Schuster. https://www.simonandschuster.com/books/True-Gretch/Gretchen-Whitmer/9781668072318